MENTAL MODELS AND THE
INTERPRETATION OF ANAPHORA

Mental models and the interpretation of anaphora

Alan Garnham

*Laboratory of Experimental Psychology,
School of Biological Sciences,
University of Sussex, UK*

PSYCHOLOGY PRESS
Taylor & Francis Group
ALERE FLAMMAM

First published 2001 by Psychology Press Ltd
27 Church Road, Hove, East Sussex, BN3 2FA

www.psypress.co.uk

Simultaneously published in the USA and Canada
by Taylor & Francis Inc.
325 Chestnut Street, Suite 800, Philadelphia, PA 19106

Psychology Press is part of the Taylor & Francis Group

© 2001 by Psychology Press Ltd

British Library Cataloguing in Publication Data
A catalogue record for this book is available from the British Library

Library of Congress Cataloging-in-Publication Data

Garnham. Alan, 1954–
    Mental models and the interpretation of anaphora / Alan Garnham.
        p. cm.—(Essays in cognitive psychology, ISSN 0959–4779)
    Includes bibliographical references and indexes.
    ISBN 1–84169–128–3
        1. Anaphora. 2. Psycholinguistics. I. Title. II. Series.

P299.A5 G37 2000
401′.9—dc21
                                                        00–05925

ISBN 1–84169–128–3

Cover design by Code 5 Design Associates Limited
Typeset by RefineCatch Limited, Bungay, Suffolk
Printed and bound in the UK by TJ International Ltd, Padstow, Cornwall

Contents

To Wendy, Robin, and Tom

Preface

This book was originally conceived in 1991 as a vehicle for integrating various strands of work on anaphor interpretation from my own laboratory both with each other and with the more general literature on this topic. It was also intended to show that the notion of a mental model is essential in the detailed description of the processes of anaphor resolution. Although both my own work and the general literature have developed considerably in the intervening years, the general thrust of the book remains the same.

My own work on mental models, some of which is described in this book, has been supported primarily by the Economic and Social Research Council (UK), grants RC00232439 ("Mental models and the interpretation of anaphora"), and R000236481 ("Mental models in text comprehension: Constraints on inference") to Alan Garnham and Jane Oakhill. It has also been supported by NATO Collaborative Research Grant CRG.890527 ("A cross-linguistic study of anaphora interpretation", and by Acción Integrada MDR/980/2/(1994/5)/532 ("Mental models and gender stereotyping in English and Spanish: A study of the relation between the availability of information and its incorporation into the mental representation of a text") from the British Council and the Spanish Ministry of Education and Science. Much of this work has been a collaborative effort and in addition to Jane Oakhill I would like to thank Kate Cain, Manolo Carreiras, Marcelle Crinean, Hannah Cruttenden, Marie-France Ehrlich, Morton Ann Gernsbacher, David Reynolds, Jools Simner, Matt Traxler, and Carolyn Wilshire for their part in it.

I would also like to thank the members of my 1999 psycholinguistics discussion group (Vivie Antonopoulou, Kate Cain, Marcelle Crinean, Sarah McCallum, Jane Oakhill, David Reynolds and Jools Simner) for their comments on the various chapters of this book. In particular, I would like to thank Kate Cain who read the entire manuscript, and with whom I had several fruitful discussions about the structure of the book. Francis Cornish, now at the Université de Toulouse-le Mirail, also provided helpful comments on the manuscript.

I would like to thank Peter Gordon and Tony Sanford, who read the manuscript for Psychology Press. I agreed with their comments, and I am sorry that I did not have the time or the space to do justice to the broader issues that they raised. Finally, thanks to the staff at Psychology Press for their patience in waiting nearly a decade for the manuscript. I hope it has been worth waiting for.

Alan Garnham
Brighton, May 2000

CHAPTER ONE

Introduction

In what remains for many the paradigm of successful research in cognitive science, David Marr (1982) put forward a theory of visual processing within a general framework for theories in that discipline. An important aspect of Marr's position is that a cognitive system has to be analysed at three levels: computational theory, representation and algorithm, and implementation. The computational theory is derived by analysing the task or tasks that the system has to perform. It specifies the (mathematical) function that the system computes, the reason it computes that function, and the constraints that allow the function to be computed given inputs that, by themselves, would typically underspecify the output. The representation and algorithm specify the abstract machinery that computes the function identified in the computational theory. The implementation specifies the physical machinery that performs the computations, and how it does so. Thus, if the human cognitive system is compared to a computer system, these three levels correspond roughly to a specification for a program, a software implementation of that specification, and the hardware on which the program runs.

In describing a computational theory for human vision, Marr tends to focus on the "what" of visual processing, though he does give some hints about his answer to the "why". For those aspects of visual processing that he analysed, Marr identified the overall purpose of visual processing as creating and updating a three-dimensional representation of the current state of part of the external world, to guide movement through, and interaction with that part of the world. Although, in a complex organism such as a human being, not every instance of visual processing fulfils this purpose (e.g., admiring a view across a beautiful landscape), it is clear what it means to say the visual system has this purpose. Marr also identified many of the constraints imposed by the world (e.g., that surfaces tend to be continuous) that the visual system uses in working out what it is currently seeing.

The topic of the present book is not vision, but text comprehension. More specifically it is about the interpretation of anaphoric expressions in texts, such as definite and indefinite pronouns, and elliptical verb phrases. Nevertheless, Marr's lessons are general ones. So, when text comprehension is studied by cognitive scientists they should expect to engage in task analysis and to formulate computational theories of what the language understanding system does, why it does those things, and what general constraints it uses. Just as in the domain of vision, it is easier to specify the "what" of the computational theory of language understanding than the "why". At least part of the answer to the "what" questions is as follows. Readers and listeners construct representation of parts of worlds. These worlds include the real world for factual texts such as newscasts, biographies, and the giving of directions, fictional worlds for novels and other literary texts, and abstract worlds for mathematical, scientific, and some aspects of, for example, political and economic discourse. In conversation, the current situation, including mental and other states of other participants must also be represented (see Johnson-Laird & Garnham, 1980).

Constructing representations of the world is not the only thing that people do in understanding what is said to them and what they read. To give one obvious example, language, and particularly spoken language, enables people to establish and develop social relations with one another. More generally, what van Dijk and Kintsch (1983) and their followers have called *situation models* are only one part, albeit an important one, of the mental representations that people construct to understand discourse and text. However, in the domain on which this book focuses, the interpretation of anaphoric expressions, the construction of a representation of part of a world is a central component of the processes under study.

A further aspect of comprehension is that people need to construct models of the (linguistic properties of the) text that they are reading or the discourse in which they are engaging. For example, to decide whether to use a feminine pronoun ("elle") or a masculine pronoun ("il") a French speaker may need to remember whether an object was referred to as a table ("la table"—feminine) or as a piece of furniture ("le meuble"—masculine). To take another example, an English speaker may need to recall whether a previous clause was active or passive, to decide whether an ellipsis (the missing material after "Bill has" in 1.1 or 1.2) means that Bill has spoken to Mary as in 1.1, or that John has spoken to Bill, as in 1.2.

(1.1)   John has spoken to Mary, and Bill has too.

(1.2)   Mary has been spoken to by John, and Bill has too.

So, although a basic finding in psycholinguistic research is that representations of the form of texts are short lived, it is essential that they are constructed and maintained to allow longer-lasting representations of content to be set up.

Turning to the "why" question, it is difficult to say, in general, what the purpose of understanding a text is. Furthermore, as with vision, any precise formulation is unlikely to cover every instance of comprehension. None the less, it would be defeatist to say that there is no general specification that captures the primary purpose of comprehension. A first suggestion might be that the reason people build mental representations of parts of worlds, real or imaginary, abstract or concrete, is to help them to make sense of the real world (including the social world), and to guide their actions and interactions in it.

As for general constraints on text comprehension, some come from properties of language and others from what is probable, given what is known about how the world works. Many of these constraints, particularly those of the second type are *soft* constraints. Language allows the description of implausible as well as plausible situations. So, for example, in 1.3, the linguistic properties of the sentence have to take precedence over general knowledge (that dogs bite men more than men bite dogs) in determining the meaning of the sentence.

(1.3)   The dog was bitten by the man.

This book attempts to set out some of the considerations, both theoretical and empirical, that determine the form of an account of anaphoric processing within a cognitive science framework. The rest of the book is structured as follows. Chapter 2 considers the components from which mental models are constructed. Chapter 3 introduces mental models theory as a psycholinguistic theory of text processing, and in particular how that theory might apply to anaphor resolution. Chapter 4 outlines the relevant linguistic literature on anaphora, and Chapters 5 and 6 describe psycholinguistic research on understanding anaphoric expressions; Chapter 5 reviews methodological issues, and Chapter 6 deals with empirical research, focusing on those aspects that are not taken up in detail in later chapters. Chapters 7 through to 10 discuss in detail research on four topics that have been the particular focus of my own work: deep and surface anaphors, anaphoric islands, implicit causality, and social stereotypes. Chapter 11 summarises the mental models account of anaphor interpretation.

CHAPTER TWO

Mental models: Their nature and construction

In the previous chapter it was suggested that a central component of the mental representation of a text is a representation of part of a world, either the real world or an imaginary world. This chapter considers the nature of these representations, and in particular the question of what components they are built from.

The representations that people build when they are reading texts can be called *mental models*. A computational theory of language understanding must specify both what such mental models are like and how they are constructed. A core part of a mental model represents part of the real or an imaginary world. So, to answer the question "What kinds of thing are represented in mental models?" it is first necessary to answer the question "What kinds of thing are there in the world?". This question is, in part, a philosophical one. However, since language is used to talk about the world, answers to this question have informed both formal and informal approaches to linguistic semantics. Semantic theory, in turn, bears on psycholinguistic theories of comprehension, because the point of comprehension is to extract the meaning (or information) conveyed by an utterance, or set of utterances, in its context.

A formal approach to semantics has much to recommend it. In particular, at the level of the individual clause, formal semantic theories show, via their links with syntax, how an interpretation of a clause can be constructed from the meaning of the words in it, and the syntactic structure that relates the words to one another (see, e.g., Cann, 1993 for an account). The formal approach can also be extended to interclause relations, and hence to aspects of discourse structure (e.g., Asher, 1993).

FORMAL SEMANTICS

The introduction of a rigorous formal approach to natural language semantics is associated in particular with the logician Richard Montague. The paper of Montague's that has been most influential in linguistic semantics is "The Proper Treatment of Quantification in Ordinary English" (Montague, 1973, usually referred to as *PTQ*). In *PTQ* Montague proposed that the semantics of English expressions can be specified by first translating English into a logical language, called IL (= intensional logic), which itself has a well-specified semantics. However, Montague regarded the intermediate language IL as a mere convenience and in other works (e.g., Montague, 1970) he suggested that the semantics of a language such as English could be specified directly.

Basic semantic types: Entities and truth values

Montague's approach requires a direct answer to the question raised earlier (what kinds of thing are there in the world?). The reason is that expressions in IL (and hence in English) have *semantic types*, which reflect the kinds of thing to which they refer. These types should, if Montague's analysis is correct, bear a close relation to the kinds of things represented in mental models.

The first part of Montague's answer is unsurprising. Texts are about individuals, in a broad sense that includes animals, objects, places, and so on, as well as people. Hence, one of Montague's fundamental semantic types is the type of entities (or individuals), just as one of the fundamental components of mental models is representations of individuals. In Montague's terminology, an expression that stands for an individual, a proper name for example, is said to be of type e (for entity), and its occurrence in a text should introduce an individual into a mental model or refer to one that is already represented in that model.

The other part of Montague's answer is more surprising, given that we talk (and write) not only about individuals, but also about properties of those individuals, and events in which they engage. Montague's system has just one other fundamental semantic type, which he calls t, the type of truth values (of which there are only two, true and false). In Montague's scheme a (declarative) sentence would be of type t. One thing that makes Montague's claim surprising is that people do not think of themselves, or the sentences they utter, as referring to truth values, but as making statements that are true or false. Nevertheless, it is important to know, and to represent mentally, whether a claim is true or false. Although some mental models might simply be representations of situations, with their veracity represented only implicitly, more complex mental models will need to represent explicitly whether claims are true or false, and who takes them to be so. Montague's idea that there is a fundamental semantic type of true values, and the idea that a psycholinguistic theory of comprehension requires a similar notion, is not as counterintuitive as it might at first appear.

If Montague's scheme is given an ontological interpretation, he is saying that the world is made up of individuals and truth values. This idea is controversial, both for what Montague includes among the basic semantic types and for what he does not. On the one hand, although people have to assess truth and falsity, the claim that truth values are one of the basic constituents of the world is not one that everybody would readily assent to. On the other hand, in Montague's scheme both events and properties are derivative, in the sense that they are analysed as being constructed out of entities and truth values. There is no basic semantic type of events, and no basic semantic type of properties, even though a prima facie case can be made for thinking that representations of events and properties are basic components of mental models.

Properties

As already indicated, the most obvious omissions from Montague's list of basic semantic types are properties and events. For reasons that will become clearer later, Montague's focus on single sentences meant that he largely failed to consider the facts that suggest that events are a fundamental semantic type. However, even within sentences, properties are ascribed to individuals, for example by the use of adjectives (e.g., "the red book"), relative clauses ("the book that my mother recommended to me"), and predicates in general ("The book felt heavy"). Montague did not deny the existence of properties, but regarded the semantic type of properties as derived, rather than basic.

To show how Montague treated properties, it is necessary to introduce the recursive rules that allow non-basic semantic types to be constructed from basic ones. There are two such rules, 2.1 and 2.2, which have different roles.

(2.1)   If A and B are types, <A,B> is a type.

(2.2)   If A is a type, <s,A> is a type.

The first rule introduces new types for expressions that do not refer to individuals or truth values. Technically, an expression of type <A,B> is a (mathematical) function from expressions of type A to expressions of type B. Put more simply, an expression of type <A,B> will combine with an expression of type A to form an expression of type B. Expressions combine with one another syntactically to form larger expressions (phrases and clauses, for example). This rule describes the semantic counterpart of syntactic combination.

The first rule is the one that allows Montague to treat properties as a derived semantic type. However, before his account is presented the function of the second rule will be explained. The second rule allows the so-called *intensional* version of each type to be created. The notion of intension is an essential part of Montague's treatment of English, as can be inferred from the fact that he used an intensional logic to capture the semantic properties of English expressions. It can be seen as a further part of his apparatus for handling truth and falsity.

The basic idea is that any expression can be used not only to describe (some aspect of) the current state of affairs in the real world, but other states of affairs, for example in the past, in the future, in an imaginary world, or in the world as someone else believes it to be. Thus, a sentence of English, such as 2.3, is not really of type t, but of type $<s,t>$. That is to say, the sentence is not simply true or false, but true in some states of affairs (possible worlds, to use the technical term) and false in others.

(2.3)   John seeks a unicorn.

Correspondingly, its semantic value is not a truth value but a mapping (or function) from states of affairs to truth values: something that tells us, for each state of affairs, whether the sentence is true or false in that state of affairs. Similarly, an expression that refers to an individual (e.g., "the man standing in the corner") may pick out one individual in one state of affairs and another individual in a different state of affairs.

To show how properties are derived from entities and truth values, questions about intensions can be ignored, and only the real world need be considered. However, mental models must use some counterpart of possible worlds, since the claims that people make have to be assessed with respect to particular worlds (the real world, fictional worlds, the world as the person addressed believes it is, and so on). Staying with the simpler case of the real world, the operation of Montague's first rule can be described. Since e and t are types $<e,t>$ is a type. The semantic value of expressions of type $<e,t>$ maps individuals to truth values. An expression of this type can be thought of as expressing a property (of individuals). Each individual either has the property and is mapped to true, or does not have the property and is mapped to false. Two classes of English expression, intransitive verbs and common nouns, have this semantic type in Montague's scheme. A common noun, such as "unicorn", divides the set of individuals into two subsets: those that are unicorns and those that are not. In other words, it assigns a truth value of true to those individuals to which it applies (in a particular state of affairs), and a truth value of false to those to which it does not. In the real world no individuals are unicorns, so the meaning of "unicorn" maps all individuals to false. Similarly, an intransitive verb, such as "walks", divides individuals into those that are walking in a particular state of affairs and those that are not.

The term *property* can be extended to cover the meanings of all expressions of the type $<A,t>$ (strictly, $<s,<A,t>>$), where A is any type. In the previous example A was e, the type of individuals, so that $<e,t>$ is the type of properties of individuals. But things other than individuals can have properties: sets, or propositions, for example, and even properties themselves.

Events

The term *event* is often used by semanticists in a broad sense, in which it covers not only events in the everyday sense, but acts, actions, states, and processes. An alternative name is *eventuality*, with the term event being reserved for all types of eventuality except states. The principal distinction between events and states is that events culminate, whereas states simply hold. In what follows, the term event will be used in the broadest sense, in which it includes states. In this sense, an event is typically described by a clause, and the type of the event and the number and nature of its participants are determined by the finite verb in the clause. This notion of an event has no place in Montague's system. On the one hand, sentences denote truth values, and on the other hand, verbs have different semantic types according to their combinatorial properties. As discussed earlier, for Montague, intransitive verbs are of type $<s,<e,t>>$, and denote properties of individuals. Transitive verbs are of the type $<s,<e,<e,t>>>$, and denote relations between (pairs of) individuals.

Montague's approach to natural language semantics can be traced back via Tarski to Frege, the founding father of modern formal logic. Frege's primary concern was with predicate calculus, in which individual sentences can be analysed separately, since there is no such thing as discourse. In under-graduate logic courses, students are usually taught that an English verb trans-lates into an n-place predicate in predicate calculus, where n is the number of individuals that are related by the type of event denoted by the verb. So the sentence 2.4 translates as 2.5.

(2.4) John loves Mary

(2.5) loves(John, Mary)

Since Montague's IL is an extension of predicate calculus, this analysis underlies his treatment of verbs as expressing relations between individuals.

However, other semanticists of the same general persuasion as Montague have argued that this approach is inadequate when discourse is considered. In an influential article, "The Logical Form of Action Sentences", Davidson (1967) pointed out that, on this scheme, a sentence such as 2.6 would naturally translate as 2.7.

(2.6)   John loves Mary dearly

(2.7)   loves(John, Mary, dearly)

From a logical point of view, this conversion of a two-place predicate into a three-place predicate complicates the statement of why "John loves Mary" is true whenever "John loves Mary dearly" is true. Davidson suggested that action sentences are existential in form, and that they state the existence of an event, which is of a particular kind (e.g., loving), and of which properties (e.g., dearly) can be predicated. More formally, 2.6 is analysed as 2.8.

(2.8) $(\exists e)[\text{loves}(e, \text{John}, \text{Mary}) \ \& \ \text{dearly}(e)]$

In this scheme, unlike Montague's, events are one of the basic semantic types.

Parsons (1990) elaborates the argument for the Davidsonian analysis of action sentences, introducing three additional types of evidence in its favour. The first relates to the analysis of so-called *perceptual idioms*, such as 2.9.

(2.9)   Sam heard Mary shoot Bill.

According to Parsons, the natural analysis of sentences of this type is one in which one event (the shooting) is the object of another (the hearing). Second, Parsons claims that the Davidsonian analysis provides a natural explanation of the relation between nominal and verbal references to events ("the singing of the *Marseillaise*" and "the *Marseillaise* was sung"). Third, Parsons points out that the analysis readily accommodates explicit quantification over events and arguments based on such quantification, as in 2.10, for example.

(2.10)   In every burning, oxygen is consumed
           Agatha burned the wood.
SO,   Oxygen was consumed.

Events bring their *participants* into relations with one another. But events themselves are also related to one another. These relations are described or implied in texts, and must be represented in mental models. This view naturally leads to the idea that representations of events, as well as representations of individuals, are basic components of mental models.

Temporal relations between events

One reason why Montague did not concern himself with such relations was that he attempted, initially, to analyse single clause sentences (and primarily sentences in the present tense). He would, nevertheless, have been aware that formal logicians, and in particular Prior (see the papers collected in Prior, 1968), had already begun to think about the problems of formalising the semantics of tense and temporal reference in natural languages. One crucial idea dates back to Reichenbach (1947). Reichenbach argued that a proper account of tenses required the identification of *three* different times, though for simple tenses two or more of these times might be the same. The three times are the utterance time, the reference time, and the event time. Consider an English pluperfect sentence, such as 2.11.

  (2.11) John had been eating.

If someone utters this sentence, it must be understood as referring to a time in the past (the reference time) before which an event of John's eating was taking place (at the event time). Furthermore, the reference time must be before the time that the sentence was uttered, if the sentence is true.

  Reichenbach's ideas apply to single clauses. Thus, to interpret each clause in a text or dialogue, it may be necessary to identify three separate times. In addition, the utterance time necessarily moves forward as a dialogue progresses, and the reference and event times may also change. Not only do the events in a narrative have a complex temporal structure, the extraction of that structure from the linguistic description of those events is not straightforward. Further complications were identified by Kamp and Reyle (1993), who propose a more complex version of Reichenbach's original theory in which five temporal indices, rather than three, are needed.

  From what has been said so far, moments of time could be a special type of entity (or individual), and be represented as such in mental models. Indeed, many attempts to provide a formal account of the meaning of tenses (so-called tense logics) were based on the idea of a *time line* made up of indefinitely many moments in a linear sequence. In most such tense logics, a past-tense sentence is true if the corresponding present-tense sentence was true at a moment before the present. Although this idea is initially plausible, it has a fatal flaw when applied to text and discourse. A sequence of past-tense sentences in a text typically denotes a sequence of events in the order they are related, as in 2.12.

  (2.12a) John came into the room.
  (2.12b) He sat down.
  (2.12c) He started to read a newspaper.

However, standard tense logic merely claims that each of these sentences should be true at some time prior to the utterance time, but says nothing about the relations between these earlier times.

In an attempt to solve this problem Kamp (1979; Kamp & Rohrer, 1983) proposed a different approach to temporal reference in which events (in the broad sense) were basic components in the interpretation of sentences. Thus, a sequence of past-tense sentences denotes a set of events in the order they are introduced. Events have finite durations. However, on Kamp's view, an event is regarded as temporally undivided when it is first introduced, though it may be divided later, for example if the following text or discourse introduces subevents of a main event. States, on the other hand, need not have a finite duration. In written French, the language that Kamp analyses, past states are typically introduced by sentences in the imperfect tense; whereas two sentences in the simple past denote two events, one following the other, a simple past followed by an imperfect denotes an event (first sentence) that took place while the state (second sentence) held. Similar observations hold for the English sentences in 2.13 and 2.14.

(2.13a)   The ship came into the harbour.
(2.13b)   It docked.

(2.14a)   The ship came into the harbour.
(2.14b)   The foghorn was sounding.

In either case, Kamp represents the relations between the events directly.

Kamp's theory is a formal semantic theory, and he takes the standard formal semantic view that a semantic analysis should state the conditions under which a text or discourse is true. His theory formalises a simple idea: A discourse is true if the relations between the events, states, and processes it denotes map in a simple way onto the relations between events, states, and processes in the real world. A description of the world itself will be more complex than what is presented in a text. An event that is effectively treated as undivided in a text will be subdivided in a richer representation. Nevertheless it is a simple matter to stipulate formally what is meant by saying that the relations in the text map onto relations in the world.

Kamp's analysis is not the last word on the logic of time and tense. Not every adjacent pair of past-tense sentences in a text describes two events, one following another. For example, world knowledge plays an important part in determining the relation between the events (e.g., Caenepeel, 1989). Consider 2.15, for example.

(2.15a)   Susan decorated the bedroom.
(2.15b)   She painted the woodwork white.

(2.15c)   She painted the walls and ceiling pale yellow.

Knowledge about decorating and about bedrooms shows that this passage does not describe three events in sequence, but one event followed by two of its subevents. However, the general approach, which takes events as fundamental semantic entities, corresponds to a plausible psycholinguistic theory in which events are basic elements of mental models.

Other relations between events

Temporal relations between events are just one type of relation that holds between them. According to Miller and Johnson-Laird (1976) the major types of relations between events are: spatial, temporal, logical, causal, intentional, and moral. If this scheme is taken as exhaustive, the category of logical relations must be construed broadly, to include the relations that hold between the parts of an argument (see, Garnham, 1991). This idea is implicit in many theories that identify coherence relations as holding between the parts of a text. Coherence relations have been given various names: combinations of predications (Longacre, 1976), rhetorical predicates (Grimes, 1975), coherence relations (Hobbs, 1983), and relational propositions (Mann & Thompson, 1986). For example, the list of relational propositions identified by Mann and Thompson is: Solutionhood, Evidence, Justification, Motivation, Reason, Sequence, Enablement, Elaboration, Restatement, Condition, Circumstance, Cause, Concession, Background, and Thesis–Antithesis. Coherence relations can be incorporated into a formal semantic theory, as in Asher's *segmented discourse representation theory* (SDRT; Asher, 1993). Whether this particular approach is correct is unclear, but again a viable psycholinguistic theory must hold that these non-temporal relations are also represented in mental models.

Representation of individual events

Events are related to one another, and their relations are represented in mental models. But how are events themselves represented? It was noted earlier that verbs, which denote types of event, are standardly mapped onto n-place predicates in predicate calculus. Although this analysis is inadequate, it does point to the fact that events bring their participants into relations with one another. One aspect of the meaning of a verb, and hence of the kind of event it denotes, is the number of participants in that event. So, an event of sleeping has one participant, one of chasing has two, and one of giving has three (the giver, the gift, and the recipient). Such information is encoded with the meaning of verbs and is used in the construction of representations of individual events (in mental models) when those verbs occur in text. However, meanings of verbs are more complex than this simple analysis implies. Individuals play different kinds of roles in events, and attempts have been made to identify sets of roles that are common to all verbs. Case grammarians (e.g., Fillmore, 1968) identified roles such as agents and instruments of action. More recently, the related notion of a thematic role has been influential both in linguistics and in psycholinguistics (see papers in Wilkins, 1988). Parsons (1990) suggests that thematic roles can be incorporated into an event-based semantic analysis, as in 2.16

(2.16) $(\exists e)[loving(e) \& agent(e,John) \& theme(e,Mary) \& dearly(e)]$

It has proved difficult to agree on a set of thematic roles, just as it proved difficult to agree on a set of cases. Nevertheless, there are arguments in favour of regarding such roles, rather than grammatical roles such as sentential subject, as contributing to the meaning of verbs. One such argument is that the same thematic role may appear, for different verbs, in different grammatical positions. For example, many interpersonal verbs can be analysed as relating a stimulus and an experiencer. However, as the comparison between 2.17 and 2.18 shows, for some verbs (e.g., "amaze") the grammatical subject (of a simple active sentence) is the stimulus and for others (e.g., "envy") it is the experiencer.

(2.17)   John amazed Bill.

(2.18)   John envied Bill.

There are other complexities to verb meanings, which will inevitably influence the way events of the kind they denote are represented in mental models (see, e.g., Pustejovsky, 1995). One that will be important in Chapter 9, is implicit causality. Many verbs describe events that are likely to have been brought about by some preceding event. That preceding event may be one in which a particular participant is the protagonist, For example, a person currently being blamed is likely to have done something blameworthy.

POSSIBLE WORLDS

Montague used the notion of a possible world to capture certain aspects of meaning, for example that a sentence such as 2.19 may be true in some situations but not in others.

(2.19)   The man with the martini waved to the hostess.

The notion of a possible world is, as its name suggests, one of an alternative to the actual world. It may share individuals with the actual world, and those individuals may have some of the properties they have in the real world. A possible world is, however, a complete world. Both in semantics and in psycholinguistics the notion of a possible world may not be the right one to capture the context dependency of interpretation. A noun phrase, such as "the table" may refer to one thing in one context (a restaurant, say) and another in a different context (at home). Semantic theories, and theories of discourse comprehension based on mental models, recognise this fact. Situation semantics (Barwise & Perry, 1983) gives situations, rather than possible worlds, a central role in an account of meaning. So, if I am in the situation of sitting with friends at a particular table in a restaurant, the noun phrase "the table" will naturally be taken as referring to the (most prominent) table in that situation. Discourse representation theory (Kamp & Reyle, 1993) postulates the construction of discourse representation structures, corresponding to the specific content of a discourse, which are used in the interpretation of the subsequent discourse, but which can be given a standard model-theoretic interpretation. Discourse representation theory is perhaps closer in spirit to mental models theory, which also suggests that models of particular discourses, taking place in particular contexts, are constructed, and that the contents of those models allow potentially ambiguous phrases, such as "the table" to be interpreted without difficulty.

SUMMARY

To decide what is represented in mental models it is necessary to consider what people talk about when they use language. One of the primary functions of language is to talk about the real world and other (imaginary) worlds. So to answer the question of what is represented in mental models, it is necessary to answer the question of what kinds of thing are in the real world and in imaginary worlds. Philosophy and linguistic semantics can suggest answers to this question. Montague, with whom the serious application of formal semantics to natural languages began, identified individuals and truth values as the two fundamental semantic types needed to analyse the semantics of certain fragments of English. Representations of individuals are clearly a central component of mental models, as is apparatus for indicating the truth or falsity of claims made in discourse. Montague claimed that properties were a derived semantic type, and he had little to say about events. However, it is plausible to suggest that both properties and events are represented directly in mental models. The fact that events are related to one another in a variety of ways supports this idea.

CHAPTER THREE

Mental models and language processing

This chapter introduces mental models theory as a psychological theory, focusing on its application to language processing. Particular emphasis is given to the role of the theory in providing a framework for developing detailed accounts of the component processes of language comprehension.

THE SCOPE OF MENTAL MODELS THEORY

Chomsky (e.g., 1968) mooted the possibility of a special language faculty, largely independent of other cognitive functions. Chomsky's arguments for this faculty focused on syntax. For example, he claimed that the range of sentence structures produced by all native speakers of a language was broadly comparable, regardless of their other capabilities. Nevertheless, even if a 7-year old child has mastered most of the syntactic structures of English, that child does not talk about the same things as an adult. Many aspects of language use do depend on our other cognitive abilities. This idea is more explicitly recognised in developments of Chomsky's ideas, such as Fodor's (1983) modularity thesis, which locates syntactic processing in the language module, but other aspects of comprehension in the (non-modular) central processing system.

There could, therefore, be a theory that unifies comprehension with other aspects of cognition. The search for unified theories is regarded as *de rigueur* in fundamental particle physics, which claims to be the most basic branch of science. Allen Newell (e.g., 1990) was a champion of the notion of a unified theory of cognition. He suggested that John Anderson's ACT* (act-star, 1983) was the first serious contender for such a theory, and that his own SOAR was the second. Johnson-Laird's (1983) claims for mental models theory are more modest. He aims to provide a theory of language, inference, and consciousness. This aim springs, in part, from his earlier work with George Miller (Miller & Johnson-Laird, 1976), in which they explored the relation between language and perception. Their underlying idea is an indisputable one. The world that people talk about is the same world that they perceive, and for humans the primary sense is vision. When a person looks at a scene, they see more detail than they would usually describe in words. Nevertheless, mental representations of parts of the world that people see must be compatible with representations of parts of the world that are described in text. The simplest hypothesis is that those representations are of the same form.

According to mental models theory, these representations are mental models of parts of the real world, or an imaginary world. The theory also incorporates inference, and indeed thought in a more general sense, since people do not simply perceive or talk about parts of the world, they think about them as well. As Kenneth Craik (1943) pointed out, in a precursor of mental models theory, the obvious way to characterise thinking about the world is as the manipulation of internal models of it. The account of consciousness put forward by Johnson-Laird (1983) is less directly connected with these notions, and it will not be considered further. In any case, mental models theory is intended to provide a unified account of language processing and thinking and reasoning.

In the domain of reasoning, Johnson-Laird has developed, within the mental models framework, detailed accounts of syllogistic reasoning (Johnson-Laird & Bara, 1984), propositional reasoning, including conditional reasoning (Johnson-Laird & Byrne, 1991), induction (Johnson-Laird, 1994a), and probabilistic reasoning (Johnson-Laird, 1994b). Attempts to extend the theory to everyday reasoning have been less well developed (Garnham, 1993; Johnson-Laird & Byrne, 1991). However, although language comprehension has identifiable components, such as word identification, syntactic processing, and inference making, these components contribute to all or almost all instances of text processing. They are not kinds of language processing in the same sense that syllogistic reasoning is a kind of reasoning. Furthermore, although it is possible to identify different types of text processing, for example skimming, reading for pleasure, and study reading, it does not seem appropriate to develop different accounts of these types of processing, since they have much in common. Thus, neither history nor task analysis suggests that the mental models approach to text comprehension should mirror its approach to reasoning.

MENTAL MODELS AS A FRAMEWORK FOR
DEVELOPING DETAILED SUBTHEORIES

In the domain of reasoning, mental models theory provides a general framework in which accounts of different types of reasoning can be developed, and a set of concepts from which those accounts can be constructed. Similarly, in language processing, mental models theory provides a framework in which to develop theories of the components of language comprehension. Garnham (1996) has argued that in the domain of reasoning there are alternative frameworks, and that mental models theory cannot, therefore, be the computational theory in the sense of Marr (1982; see also Chapter 1). In the domain of language, however, the most general principles of mental models theory are part of the computational theory—they result from an analysis of what comprehension is. Examples of these principles are that texts convey information from one person to another and that (part of) this information is about situations in the real or an imaginary world.

THE SYMBOLIC NATURE OF
MENTAL MODELS THEORY

In recent years, connectionist accounts of language processing have attracted much interest. This approach has had its greatest successes in the domain of word identification. More particularly, it has been most successful in accounting for the effects of regularities, such as those in spelling to sound systems, that are hard to capture by sets of rules but that reflect probabilistic patterns of association. Given the mechanisms of pattern recognition that are incorporated into connectionist networks, these facts are not surprising. However, even in the domain of word identification, connectionist models have difficulty in accounting for the acquisition of regularities that are rule based (see, e.g., Pinker, 1993). Furthermore, connectionism does not provide a framework for describing rule-based processes. Neither does it provide an obvious way of describing the structured representations needed to capture the form and content of text. Mental models theory is, therefore, formulated symbolically, and, to the extent that it has been incorporated into computer models, those models have also been symbolic models.

ASSUMPTIONS OF MENTAL MODELS THEORY

The guiding assumption of mental models theory is that the representations people construct when perceiving the world, when hearing and reading about it, and when thinking about it, are representations of situations. When people find out about, or think about, the real world, those representations are representations of situations in the real world. But people also construct representations of situations in imaginary worlds, for example fictional worlds, wished-for worlds, and the world as other people believe it to be.

In the domain of reasoning, mental models theory contrasts with accounts that assume people reason by transforming sentences expressing what they already know into other sentences, using formal rules. Formal rules are rules whose application is determined by only the form of the sentences to which they apply, and not by their content. Such theories are not, therefore, primarily concerned with the way that people represent the world. A prototypical piece of reasoning of this kind would be one based on the rule of *modus ponens*. This rule says that from two sentences, the first of the form "P", and the second of the form "if P then Q", a third sentence of the form "Q" can be derived. As long as P is the same in both sentences, the conclusion Q follows. Whether it is true depends, in addition, on whether P itself is true, and whether it is true that if P then Q.

It is likely that people sometimes reason in this way. They can certainly learn abstract rules (Smith, Langston, & Nisbett, 1992). However, it is unlikely that all or even a significant part of our everyday reasoning makes use of such rules. Indeed, even for more formal reasoning, Johnson-Laird has shown in a variety of studies (e.g., Johnson-Laird, Byrne, & Schaeken, 1992) that the predictions of a mental models-based theory are more accurate than those of a theory based on formal rules.

In the domain of language processing, mental models theory might also appear to contrast with theories that analyse comprehension as the extraction of a representation of the form of sentences, rather than their content. However, such a theory is not obviously a theory of comprehension, since task analysis shows that comprehension is not the extraction of sentence form. An early psycholinguistic theory claiming that the primary purpose of language comprehension was to produce a mental representation of the linguistic properties of a text was the *derivational theory of complexity* (as the theory inherent in George Miller's early psycholinguistic studies was later dubbed). This theory and its successors (e.g., Fodor, Bever, & Garrett, 1974) claimed that sentences are represented by their syntactic deep structure. Although this representation is syntactic, deep structure contains all the information necessary to compute meaning, according to the 1965 version of Chomsky's theory. Within linguistics, this idea led to the byzantine proposals for deep structures of the generative semanticists, who sought, for example, to include information about the illocutionary force of sentences (whether they were intended as descriptions, commands, promises, etc.) into deep structure (e.g., Sadock, 1974).

It was in reaction to this theory that Bransford (e.g., Bransford, Barclay, & Franks, 1972; Bransford & Franks, 1971) proposed a precursor of the mental models theory. Bransford pointed out one fundamental limitation of the deep structure approach, namely that it is *sentences* that have deep structures, so that the only account of discourse meaning in theories of this kind is that the meaning of a text is a concatenation of sentence meanings. As Bransford realised, and as semanticists of all types have explicitly acknowledged since, texts have meanings over and above the meanings of the sentences in them.

Another theory of language comprehension with which mental models theory has been contrasted, is a theory based on propositional representations. The notion of a proposition, as the meaning of a sentence (perhaps relativised to a context of use) is originally a philosophical one. However, the term propositional representation was taken up in the late 1960s, in both psychology and artificial intelligence, to describe a quasi-standardised way of writing down representations of sentences and, supposedly, the meanings carried by them. The notation was based loosely on the predicate–argument format used in predicate calculus, though questions about quantification were frequently ignored, or glossed over. In retrospect, systems of propositional representation provided little more than an alternative language for writing down things that could be expressed in English (or another natural language). Because of their simplified syntax, as compared with natural languages, they were easy for computer programs to manipulate. This simplified syntax derived partly from their source in predicate calculus and partly from the fact that they had no apparatus for capturing many nuances of meaning.

Many propositional representations bear a strong resemblance to the sentences whose meanings they represent, and a theory of comprehension based on propositional representations might be thought of as another version of the theory that comprehension is the extraction of (a regimented version of) linguistic form. Indeed, given that psycholinguists have long recognised that superficial aspects of texts are remembered at least for short periods, Johnson-Laird (e.g., 1982) proposed that propositional representations might be one such superficial representation, and that they might be constructed as an intermediate stage in the derivation of mental models. This view is problematic, for several reasons (see Sanford & Garrod, 1998). Nevertheless, it emphasises the connection between propositional representations and superficial ones, a link that is important in the present context because much of the information in the superficial representations of a text is information about linguistic structure.

Johnson-Laird (1983) identified two other general properties of mental models: They must be finite, and they should be computable. Mental models must be finite in the apparently trivial sense that they have to fit inside people's heads. However, there are two reasons why this assumption is not entirely trivial. First, people are able to represent infinite quantities. Infinite quantities can readily be given finite representations, most obviously using the mathematical symbol for infinity (∞). Second, in many versions of formal semantics, meanings of expressions are represented as infinite sets (or their equivalent functions). These sets are usually specified by enumerating a few members, and indicating that the sets have infinitely more members of the same kind. For example, the meaning of a common noun, such as dog, might be characterised as a function from possible worlds to sets of individuals, where each set is the set of dogs in the corresponding possible world. However, without enumeration of the sets of dogs, this definition is useless, since it uses the notion of dog in the specification of the component sets. Even if mental models theory needs to borrow ideas from formal semantics, which it undoubtedly does, it cannot postulate that the representation of the meaning of every content word is infinite.

In fact, formal semanticists use the notion of enumeration only to finesse the question of, for example, what makes a dog a dog. The idea is that, if it were known what makes something a dog, it would be possible to say in any situation (or possible world) which things are dogs and which are not (i.e., to specify the sets of dogs without enumerating them). Thus, enumerated sets are stand-ins for meanings, and semanticists use them when they are not interested in the meanings of words themselves, but in how those meanings combine. For this purpose a set-theoretic (or functional) representation of meaning is essential, but an extensional (or enumerative) view of set membership is not.

The idea that mental models should be computable derives from the fact that people do not have a pre-stored representation of every situation they might encounter, hear about, read about, or think about. There are complex mechanisms for constructing mental models of situations from descriptions of them in discourse and text, and a mental models theory of comprehension must specify these mechanisms. For simple texts, people can presumably construct appropriate models. However, there may be cases, for example in everyday reasoning (see, Garnham, 1993; Johnson-Laird & Byrne, 1991, chap. 9) in which the correct model is not computable. These cases will be ones in which people's reasoning might be expected to fail.

Mental models and language processing

In addition to the general assumptions of mental models theory, there are some assumptions that are particular to the theory as applied to language processing. The first is that mental models are constructed incrementally. This assumption must be made because readers and listeners understand texts and discourse as they go along. They do not have to wait to the end of a text before they begin to understand it. Indeed, even within a sentence, processing is incremental (see, e.g., Marslen-Wilson, 1973, 1975). The assumption, or rather the fact, of incremental processing means that, as a theory of comprehension is worked out within the mental models framework, the detailed mechanisms that extract information from the current piece of text, and add it to the model so far, will have to be specified.

A more specific assumption, again derived partly from observation of how comprehension works, is that the model of the text constructed so far forms part of the context for the interpretation of the current text. This interpretation then updates the model, and changes the context for interpreting the next piece of text (Isard, 1975). In developing a mental models theory of comprehension, it is important to specify exactly how the model so far acts as a context for interpreting the current piece of text. One of the most important ways in which it does so, and one that is the main focus of this book, is in constraining the interpretation of anaphoric expressions. For example, the simple noun phrase "the table" is an expression that is typically used to refer to a single thing of the type table. However, there are millions of tables in the real world, and plenty of others in imaginary worlds! Without a context it is impossible to determine what table the phrase refers to. In a well-written text, however, the referent of such a noun phrase will be clear. One job of a mental model is, therefore, to provide representations of a small set of people and things, to which simple noun phrases, such as "the table" might refer. Since mental models are constructed incrementally, they can be initialised (at the beginning of a text or discourse) with little or no content, though they are not always empty at this point. A newscast, for example, updates stories in previous newscasts. In any case, a mental model can contain only those objects that are specifically introduced, in one way or another, by the text. The most obvious way in which texts introduce elements into mental models is by explicitly mentioning them. For example, a text that begins "Stately, plump Buck Mulligan . . . " introduces a male character, by the name of Buck Mulligan and with the properties of being stately and plump, into the model of the text if that character has not been introduced by the title (which he hasn't in this case) or by background knowledge (which will be true for some readers of the book in question).

There are other ways that a text can provide referents for noun phrases. For example, Clark (1977) described a range of cases that require what he calls *bridging inferences*, in which a reference to an entity is justified because that entity is related to something mentioned previously. One relation that sustains such references is part–whole, as in 3.1.

(3.1)   John bought a new car. The engine needed tuning.

Cars have one engine each, so the engine referred to in the second sentence is the engine of the car mentioned in the first sentence. For many years there has been a debate about whether these inferences are made in a forward or a backward direction. Or, rather, since Haviland and Clark (1974) showed that some are made in a backward direction, there has been a debate about whether any are made in a forward direction. The inference would be made in a forward direction if, when a car was mentioned, the existence of its engine was inferred. A backward inference would mean that the fact that the engine was part of the previously mentioned car was only inferred when the engine itself (but not its relation to the car) was mentioned. Haviland and Clark showed that a sentence such as 3.2 took longer to understand when a bridging inference was needed than when it was not.

(3.2)   The beer was warm.

They concluded, therefore, that the inference was made in the backward direction.

Forward inferencing is possible because people have detailed (if mundane) knowledge about, for example, cars—about their main parts, about how to drive them, about the law as it relates to cars and driving, and so on. The question is, when someone represents a car in a mental model, do they represent it as a car and nothing else, or is background knowledge used to elaborate the model? For example, if someone represented not only a car, but the parts that they knew it must have, that would be equivalent to making forward inferences, such as that this particular car has an engine.

Mental models theory emphasises that, whatever the direction of the inference, it is the inference that this specific car has its own specific engine. Making this inference is not the same as having a piece of information (the general fact that cars have engines) available in memory when reading about cars. The distinction is particularly important when considering the interpretation of probe word experiments. Thus, if responses to "engine" are quicker than expected after reading 3.3, it might be because a (forward) inference had been made that this particular car has a particular engine, and the engine might be represented in the mental model of the text.

(3.3)   John bought a new car.

However, it might mean that in processing the *word* "car", while constructing a mental model of John buying a new car, general knowledge about cars had been activated, because of the way that knowledge is connected to the word "car" in long-term memory. Knowledge about cars includes the information that cars have engines, and that information in turn is connected to a representation of the word "engine". It may be that these connections, and not an inference, speed responses to "engine".

The question of what entities are introduced into mental models by particular expressions in a text, and hence of what forward inferences are made, is one that will be returned to at several points in this book. Several suggestions have been made, though they are not always easy to test empirically. Two of these ideas, which embody different approaches to the problem, will be discussed here.

Garrod and Sanford (1981) showed that some sentences that appear to need bridging inferences for their interpretation are understood just as quickly as when bridging inferences are not required. They compared, for example, 3.4a followed by 3.4c with 3.4b followed by 3.4c.

(3.4a)   Mary dressed the baby.
(3.4b)   Mary put the clothes on the baby.
(3.4c)   The clothes were made of pink wool.

One reason 3.4a might introduce a set of clothes into the mental model, which "the clothes" in 3.4c could refer to, is that the definition of the verb "dress" has clothes as a component. Thus, when the definition of "dress" is used to build a representation of a specific act of dressing, that specific act has a specific set of clothes as a component.

A different account of forward inferencing derives from the intuition that some connections are so obvious that people cannot help making them. A recent version of this idea is found in McKoon and Ratcliff's (1992) minimalist theory of inference during reading. McKoon and Ratcliff claim that the only inferences people make automatically when they are reading are those required for local cohesion (usually bridging inferences made in a backward direction) and those based on readily available knowledge. If this theory is to have explanatory power, "readily available" must be defined in a way that is both plausible and consistent with known facts, while avoiding circularity. For example, several studies suggest that when people read a sentence about sweeping the yard, they do not infer that a broom was used. The theory is thus committed to the claim that the knowledge that brooms are used to sweep yards is not readily available. If this claim can be based on an independently motivated definition of ready availability, the theory is safe. If the claim is made simply because it has to be made to save the theory, the value of the theory needs to be reconsidered.

BRANSFORD'S THEORY OF LANGUAGE UNDERSTANDING

As mentioned earlier, John Bransford pointed out that the mental representation of the content of a text is not the same as a representation of its linguistic form, at any level of linguistic description. One of his reasons for making this claim was that the meaning of a text is not just a string of sentence meanings. Information from the different sentences and clauses of a text must be *integrated*, not merely concatenated. Bransford did not present a detailed account of integration, but the making of bridging inferences is one aspect of integration. And it is just one component process in the interpretation of anaphoric expressions, the topic of this book.

Another aspect of comprehension that Bransford stressed is its constructive aspect. By saying that comprehension is a constructive process, Bransford meant that the meaning of a text must be put together from two sources. The first is the information that is explicit in the text, and the second is related information in the reader's or listener's long-term memory. As has already been shown, bridging inferences often rely on background information, so the integrative and constructive aspects of comprehension are often inter-dependent. Thus, as pointed out by Garnham (1992), McKoon and Ratcliff (1992) were wrong to oppose their minimalist theory to what they call con-structionist theories. Minimal inferences required for local cohesion often depend on constructive processes.

Although the integrative and constructive aspects of comprehension are often linked, they are conceptually distinct. Integration may depend only on linguistic conventions, not on background knowledge. For example, if 3.5b follows 3.5a, the identification of the individual referred to as "the man" in the second sentence with the individual introduced by the indefinite "a man" in the first depends only on knowledge about how definite and indefinite noun phrases work.

(3.5a)   A man and a woman entered the room.
(3.5b)   The man was wearing a green hat.

Similarly, construction is possible without integration, and has been called the making of *merely elaborative inferences*. The forward inferences discussed earlier are merely elaborative, even though they might be useful later for integration. If someone infers the existence of the car's engine, when they read "John bought a new car", they have no guarantee that the engine will be mentioned, and hence no guarantee that their inference will help integration. But if the engine is mentioned, the inference can aid integration at that point.

Bransford believed that people make many elaborative inferences while they are reading. However, his evidence came from experiments in which he examined memory for the content of a text. He, therefore, failed to exclude the possibility that the questions in his memory tests induced the elabor-ations. Later research supported this alternative explanation of his results. For example, as mentioned earlier, people appear not to infer highly probable instruments for actions (such as a shovel for digging a hole). Nevertheless, it was once thought that they did, because "shovel" is a good memory cue for a sentence about digging a hole (Paris & Lindauer, 1976). The crucial study that showed this interpretation to be wrong was that of Corbett and Dosher (1978). Corbett and Dosher replicated the main result, but in addition showed that "shovel" was a good cue for any sentence about digging a hole. In particular they showed it was a good cue for a sentence about digging a hole with a pitchfork (an improbable instrument), even though people remembered that the actual instrument was a pitchfork. Thus, Corbett and Dosher undermined the argument that "shovel" was a good cue for a sentence about digging a hole (with no instrument mentioned) because the existence of a specific shovel used in the specific event of digging a hole had been inferred and encoded into its representation.

As mentioned earlier, the question of forward inferencing, and hence of constructive processing that is not linked to integration, is an open one. However, the question of whether constructive processing occurs is not. Constructive processing is a crucial part of comprehension. Mental models theory shows how this processing can take place. Mental models are representations of parts of the real or of an imaginary world. Background knowledge is also knowledge about the real or imaginary world. Mental models and world knowledge have the same form, and hence there is no difficulty in fitting together representations constructed from explicit information in a text, and information from long-term memory.

One minor qualification must be added to this last remark. Background knowledge can either be knowledge about specifics or knowledge about generalities. Texts too can be about specifics or generalities. One common use of background knowledge is the use of knowledge of generalities to fill in details about specific individuals. For example, in the passage about the car and its engine, the general knowledge that cars have engines (and that they have one each) allows the specific reference to the engine of an already identified car. This process is a straightforward one. Representations of types of objects (cars, for example) are abstractions from representations of specific objects. Thus, a representation of a specific car can be created from a general template for cars, by filling in details specific to that car, by inheriting details that apply to all cars, or to all cars by default (i.e., if there is no information to the contrary—occasionally one comes across a car without an engine). However, making a fleshed-out copy of a general car representation is not enough. Something, perhaps an explicit aspect of the representation, perhaps the way it is used, must indicate that this is *a representation of an individual*, and not a representation of cars in general.

WHAT A THEORY OF LANGUAGE PROCESSING SHOULD EXPLAIN

People use language for many reasons, and the goals of the reader or listener affect the way they process incoming linguistic information (see, e.g., Goldman, 1997). If Mary asks John the way to the station, she may try to ignore his parenthetical remarks about the state of his health that form part of his reply. Or, someone's attention may wander as they are reading a book they are not really interested in, and they may suddenly realise that they have no idea what the last few pages were about. Nevertheless, there is a common and important type of comprehension in which the reader or listener is trying to construct a coherent representation of what the writer or speaker is trying to convey. One way of characterising this type of comprehension (or perhaps component of comprehension is a better term, since it will be part of reading for deeper meaning, for example) would be to say it comprises: extracting the explicit information from the text, making whatever inferences are necessary to link the pieces of explicit information into a coherent whole, and (maybe) incorporating other inferences that are so solid or so easily made that there is no reason to avoid making them.

If this characterisation is to be useful, it is necessary to clarify (1) what is meant by the explicit content of a text, and (2) how knowledge is organised in memory so that it can be used rapidly to make bridging and other inferences. The second question is a difficult one, and will not be answered in this book. The first question is more tractable. From a mental models perspective, answering the question means specifying how parts of a model are constructed from part of the text. This book is not the place to present a detailed account of this process, since many aspects of it are not pertinent to anaphor comprehension. However, it is a process that depends intimately on syntax and semantics, sentential and discourse level. A full account would, therefore, draw in detail on the knowledge of syntax and semantics that has been systematised by syntacticians and formal semanticists (see Chapter 2).

Constructing mental models

The preceding discussion has already drawn informally on a small part of our knowledge of syntax and semantics, for example in characterising the interpretation of definite and indefinite noun phrases. Such expressions can be recognised by their form (they begin with a definite or an indefinite article, for example) and are interpreted as having meanings of certain kinds, of which one of the most important is referring to individuals and sets of individuals. The syntax and semantics of noun phrases is complex. Although singular definite noun phrases typically refer to individual entities and plural definite noun phrases to sets of such entities, there are exceptions. A singular definite noun phrase may refer to a generic type, as in 3.6, or to a set of individuals, as in 3.7.

(3.6)   The elephant is a large mammal.

(3.7)   The committee is now meeting.

If comprehension is to be possible, these exceptions must be systematically identifiable.

The syntax and semantics of noun phrases determine the kind of thing that a particular noun phrase refers to and, together with its context of use, provide strong clues to whether it refers to something previously mentioned in the discourse, and hence whether it requires a new element to be introduced into the mental model.

If noun phrases typically refer to individuals, verbs denote acts, actions, states, and processes. In formal semantics, the term event (or eventuality) is used in a general sense for things of this kind (see Chapter 2). Syntactic considerations determine, at least in part, the roles that the various protagonists, typically denoted by noun phrases, play in the event. For example, the sentential subject in a simple active sentence describing many types of event will denote the agent, or person who carried out the action, as in 3.8.

(3.8)   John bought a bunch of flowers.

References to events are complicated by their temporal properties and temporal relations, which determine the meaning of extended discourse (again, see Chapter 2). These properties and relations may be encoded grammatically, using the grammatical systems of aspect and tense. English has present and past tenses, as indicated by modifications of the root verb form (e.g., "run", "ran"), but no (grammaticalised) future tense. Future time is indicated by the root form of the verb preceded by a present tense form of the auxiliary "will" or the semi-auxiliary "be going to". Nevertheless, understanding that an event is described as taking place in the future is just as important as understanding that it is described as past or present. Events can also have aspectual properties such as being extended in time, and being repeated. These properties, too, can be grammatically encoded. For example, the distinction between French simple past and imperfect "tenses" is primarily an aspectual one. In whatever way these temporal aspects of events are conveyed in a particular language, they have to be extracted and encoded during comprehension.

Temporal relations between events can be signalled by relations between tenses, which can be formalised by sequence of tense rules (Higginbotham, 1995). These relations are sometimes anaphoric, and explicit parallels have been drawn between noun phrase anaphora and temporal anaphora (e.g., Nelken & Francez, 1997; Partee, 1984). Sequences of tense rules for multiclause sentences show that, for example, the utterance time for embedded speech, as in 3.9, may be anaphorically related to the event time of the speech itself, so that on one reading of 3.9 the event of the unicorn's walking is before the time of Mary's statement.

(3.9)   Mary said that a unicorn was walking.

Rules about temporal relations that hold between events described in separate sentences were discussed in Chapter 2.

Temporal relations can also be signalled by temporal adverbs, and by conjunctions. For example, adverbs and adverb phrases such as "soon", "yesterday", and "the week after next" specify in greater detail the relation between utterance time or event time and reference time. Conjunctions such as "while", "after", and "before" can explicitly signal the relations between events that Kamp showed could be signalled by relations between tenses. They can also override defaults, so "before A, B" places event B temporally before A, even though A is described first in the text. Comprehension processes must use these linguistic signals to construct appropriate mental models.

A description of an event can be elaborated by describing its subevents (see Chapter 2). Indeed, a large part of the skill of writing or telling stories is to divide the big events up into parts in an interesting way. Individual events can also be elaborated with adverbial modifiers. Temporal adverbs are one example, and spatial ones show some of the same indexical properties. "Here" and "there" parallel "now" and "then", for example. However, because information about spatial location is not encoded into event descriptions in the way that temporal information must be, the spatial domain is not so complex in this respect. Space does, however, have its complexities, both in the interpretation of adverb phrases of place, in particular prepositional phrases, and in the use of both object-centred and speaker-centred coordinate systems (see, e.g., Garnham, 1989a; Levelt, 1984; Miller & Johnson-Laird, 1976). These complexities will not be described here though they have consequences for the construction of mental models.

From a semantic point of view, manner adverbs are simpler than temporal and spatial ones, with the caveat that manner adverbials, like other adverbials, can be full clauses, and hence introduce new events. Manner adverbs typically specify properties of events (e.g., "John drove carefully"), just as adjectival modifiers of noun phrases specify properties of individuals. Noun phrases, like event descriptions, can take more complex modifiers, such as prepositional phrases, which place the referent of the noun phrase in relation to another individual, and relative clauses, which give the noun phrase's referent a role in another event. However, the representation of properties, even those described by single adjectives or adverbs, has its own complexities. Describing an individual as tall or good may appear simple enough, but there are well-known problems in specifying the meaning of both of these adjectives.

In summary, texts are about individuals (people, animals, objects, places, and so on). Individuals are typically introduced by noun phrases. They are also often mentioned more than once. An important part of language production is selecting the right noun phrases to refer to individuals that have already been mentioned. And an important part of comprehension lies in recognising when there is a repeated reference. Individuals have properties, most simply expressed by adjectives, and relationships to one another that can be signalled directly (e.g., "the car's engine"), or indirectly via the roles that the individuals are assigned in events by verbs. Events, too, have properties, but more importantly relations to other events that are signalled in a variety of ways.

More complexities of interpretation

The preceding subsection has only hinted at the complexities of constructing a mental model. Three further issues will be considered in this subsection, to indicate further the intricacies of the process of deriving a mental representation of the content of a text from its linguistic form. First, it has already been mentioned that definite and indefinite articles have a crucial effect on the interpretation of noun phrases (see Hawkins, 1978 for a detailed discussion). These articles are just two examples of determiners that can introduce noun phrases. Other examples include possessives (e.g., "my", "Bill's") and quantifiers (e.g., "some", "all", "many", "few", "a few", "at least six"). As Moxey and Sanford (1993) have shown, quantifiers encode quantities in an context-dependent way. In addition, they have focusing properties that affect the construction of mental models. Many of the quantifiers focus, as might be expected, on the subset of the set specified by their head noun that has the property specified by the predicate of the sentence. For example, 3.10 focuses on the authors (head noun) who hoped to win the prize (predicate).

(3.10)   Many of the authors hoped to win the prize.

This fact is reflected in the ease with which a following pronoun can refer to this set, as in 3.11.

(3.11)   They dreamed of what they would do with the prize money.

On the other hand, it is almost impossible for an immediately following "they" to refer to authors who did not hope to win the prize. What is surprising is that some quantifiers have the reverse property, "few" for example. In 3.12 "they" is most naturally taken as referring to the authors that did *not* hope to win the prize.

(3.12)   Few of the authors hoped to win the prize.
         They scorned its commercialism.

On the other hand, 3.13 sounds bizarre.

(3.13)   Few of the authors hoped to win the prize.
         They dreamed of what they would do with the prize money.

Quantifier phrases such as "many of the authors" and "few of the authors" are not themselves referring expressions, and the pronouns in 3.11 and 3.12 are not co-referential with these expressions. They refer to sets that have to be constructed from explicit information in the text. (See also the discussion of E-type pronominal references in Chapter 4.)

Second, one special kind of "individual" that people stand in relation to is a piece of information that can be conveyed linguistically. Thus, many verbs take complements that are sentential in form, and that are introduced by complementisers such as "that", "if", and "whether". Characterising the semantics of sentences about beliefs, and related *propositional attitudes*, is not an easy matter, as formal semanticists can testify. Nevertheless, representations of beliefs are an important component of mental models, partly because people talk about their own and other people's beliefs, and partly because a person's beliefs determine how information is best conveyed to them (see Johnson-Laird & Garnham, 1980).

Third, apart from the temporal conjunctions discussed previously, there are many other conjunctions, most of which indicate argumentative or rhetorical relations between pieces of information. "But", for example, draws attention to a contrast, and "because" signals a relation based on a cause, a reason, or evidence. These kinds of relation, like temporal ones, need not always be signalled explicitly. Simply juxtaposing pieces of information may indicate that they are related.

For texts that are not merely descriptive, and few interesting texts are, argumentative relations are important. A basic assumption of mental models theory is that the same situation can be described in many ways. This fact reflects Bransford's claim that representations of content do not correspond to linguistic representations. The same argument can also be presented in different ways. A theory of argument structure is, therefore, needed to specify what form mental models of arguments take. An account is also needed of how such models can be derived from texts presenting arguments. There have been many attempts to specify the structure of arguments, though there are problems with all of them. Garnham (1991) suggests that a major component of a theory of how argument structure is derived from text is a specification of the semantics of the natural language connectives that indicate argumentative or rhetoric relations, and of how statements that are not explicitly related by connectives are linked to one another. In the later case, background knowledge is important. For example 3.14 can be interpreted as indicating a causal relation because a window may break when it is hit by a stone.

(3.14)   The stone hit the window. It broke.

Conversely, if a relation is signalled linguistically, it may be possible to infer a specific relation in the real world from the type of relation signalled by the conjunction. For example, most people who are not sailors do not know about kevlar sails, their properties, or their use in different wind conditions. However, 3.15 signals that a relation based on cause, reason, or evidence holds between two pieces of information and the reader can infer that kevlar sails are good when there is little wind.

(3.15)   Connors used kevlar sails, because there was little wind.

In fact, casual readers appear not to make these inferences routinely (Noordman & Vonk, 1992), but they could if they wished.

PARTIAL INTERPRETATIONS OF A TEXT

Since comprehension is not a monolithic process, different aspects may be completed more or less quickly, or sometimes not at all. Mental models theory must be able to accommodate such partial interpretation. This section discusses two cases in which interpretation might be described as partial.

McKoon and Ratcliff (1990) suggest that inferences might be only partly encoded. One version of this idea receives some support from Gumenik (1979), who questioned Anderson et al.'s (1976) conclusion that general terms are *instantiated* when they occur in particular contexts, for example "container" as "basket" in 3.16.

(3.16)   The container held the apples.

Gumenik showed that both "architect" and "builder" were good recall cues for 3.17.

(3.17)   The man planned the house.

This result suggests that certain properties of the man are encoded from 3.17, but that these properties are not sufficient to support either the inference that he is an architect or the inference that he is a builder. The encoded properties interact with the properties of the cue word to determine how good a cue for the sentence it is. This idea partly, but not wholly, vindicates Gumenik's attempt to explain instantiation as a retrieval phenomenon.

Oakhill, Garnham, and Vonk (1989) discuss a different case in which the interpretation of a text can be described as partial. In a sentence such as 3.18 at least two types of information point to the conclusion that "she" refers to Joan: (1) the gender of the pronoun and the conventions that Joan and Stan are names for a female and a male, respectively, and (2) the fact that cycling is an alternative to driving by car, and that if you have something that you do not currently need you might lend it to someone who could make use of it.

(3.18)   Joan lent her car to Stan because she had taken up cycling.

In some sentences only one of these types of information can help to resolve a pronoun. For example, only the second type of information is useful in 3.19.

(3.19)   Joan lent her car to Sue because she had taken up cycling.

Conversely, only the first type of information is available in 3.20.

(3.20)   Joan and Sam saw each other. He waved.

When both types of information are potentially helpful, as in 3.18, either or both could be used to resolve the pronoun. Oakhill et al. describe the use of the first type of information as role-to-name mapping for the pronoun, since the referent of the pronoun (who plays the agent role in the "because" clause) is mapped onto the (referent of the) name Sam. They describe the use of the second type of information as role-to-role mapping, since the referent of the pronoun is mapped onto the person filling the role of the lendee in the main clause. If only one of these types of mapping is carried out, an incomplete representation of the information in the text may result. In a psycholinguistic experiment, where the names of the people are often arbitrary, it may be more important to effect role-to-role mapping, or at least more important to retain its results in memory.

ALTERNATIVES TO MENTAL MODELS THEORY?

If the most general principles of mental models theory are part of the computational theory of language comprehension (Garnham, 1996), there cannot be any true alternative to the theory. However, there are many other theories of comprehension in the literature, so what is their status? It was suggested earlier that some of the earlier theories of comprehension focused on the wrong question (how is the linguistic form of a text extracted and mentally represented?). However, the same claim cannot be made of more recent theories. One possibility is that mental models theory has failed to fully analyse what it is to understand discourse or text, that it does not provide a complete computational theory, and that other theories try to fill the gaps it has left. An alternative possibility is that other theories analyse comprehension at the level of representation and algorithm, that of the abstract machinery that computes the function identified in the computational theory. Marr argued that such an approach was mistaken, and that proper task analysis was essential in all branches of cognitive science. A third possibility is that other theories overlap with mental models theory and present the same or similar ideas in a different guise.

There is some truth in all of these suggestions. For example, mental models theory as presented in this chapter does not impose strong constraints on what elaborative inferences are made, or on how the reader's focus of attention changes through a text. There may be general principles that can be developed as part of a computational theory of comprehension, and that are pertinent to these issues. A related possibility is that such constraints derive from properties of memory or attentional systems that are used in comprehension and follow from the computational theories for those systems. In an empirical study of inference making, Graesser, Singer, and Trabasso (1994) attempted to identify which types of elaborative inference are made during comprehension. For example, they claimed that superordinate goal and causal antecedent inferences tend to be made, whereas subordinate goal and causal consequence inferences tend not be be. The kind of general principle that might underlie these findings is that in order to understand a narrative it is necessary to know the main characters' high-level goals.

Turning to the second possibility, it is certainly true that many theories of text comprehension place more emphasis on the details of the psychological mechanisms underlying comprehension than does mental models theory as presented here. Kinstch and van Dijk (1978), for example, describe the role of short-term (working) memory in integrating material from different parts of a text. This account effectively takes integration for granted (computational theory) and provides a model of the (abstract) machinery (representation and algorithm) needed to achieve integration. Kintsch also suggests a crucial role for the immediate construction of propositions (a particular type of representation) as a step towards comprehension. However, as Marr emphasised, a function can be computed in many different ways. An alternative account (Sanford & Garrod, 1998) suggests that links must be made directly between subpropositional parts of a text (words, for example) and background knowledge, before information is combined into a more integrated representation of the content of the text. Sanford and Garrod present a variety of evidence in favour of their account, and note that in Kintsch's (1988) more recent construction-integration model direct links to a knowledge base are made from words in the text. Other researchers have also emphasised the importance of the way information in a text accesses memory (see papers in O'Brien, Lorch, & Myers, 1998). Recent *memory-based* theories of comprehension take a particular view of this process (a fast passive process in which information in text potentially interacts with all other information in memory). However, these theories do not describe what it is to understand a text (computational theory) but focus on the mechanisms by which memory is accessed.

It would be wrong, however, to construe Sanford and Garrod's account merely as a suggestion about the representations and algorithms used in text comprehension. In a related piece of work, Sanford and Moxey (1999) suggest that mental models have properties that are somewhat different from those expected if a strong parallel is drawn between those models and the discourse representation structures of discourse representation theory. Sanford and Garrod's *scenario mapping and focus* approach places greater emphasis than the account given in this book on the use of background knowledge in comprehension, and less on the formal properties of the text. Some of the evidence they cite shows that under certain circumstances background knowledge has a stronger influence than formal properties. For example, people will answer "yes" to the question in 3.21.

(3.21)   Can a man marry his widow's sister?

They fail to notice that if a man has a widow he must be dead, and therefore cannot remarry. A psychological theory of comprehension must account for these errors, but it must also account for the fact that people can see that they are errors.

In fact, the scenario mapping and focus approach has much in common with mental models theory, and thus is an example of an approach that expresses (some of) the same ideas in a different way. The same is true of Gernsbacher's (1990) structure building framework. Indeed, the term "structure building" immediately suggests a parallel with mental models theory. Nevertheless, Gernsbacher's ideas are expressed in different terms from those of mental models theory, and she also focuses on detailed mechanisms, this time those of suppression (of less relevant information) and enhancement (of more relevant information), that are used in comprehension. As a last example, van Dijk and Kintsch (1983) introduced situation models, which bear a marked similarity to mental models, into a revised version of Kintsch and van Dijk's (1978) theory.

SUMMARY

Mental models theory is a psychological theory of language processing and reasoning. The theory provides a framework within which more detailed accounts of the component processes of comprehension and reasoning can be developed. In reasoning, these component processes are types of reasoning, such as syllogistic reasoning. In language processing, they are subprocesses such as anaphor interpretation. Mental models theories of reasoning contrast with rule-based theories. Mental models theories of comprehension have been contrasted with theories based on the extraction of the form of discourse, but such theories do not capture the essence of comprehension. It can, therefore, be argued that (some of) the basic principles of mental models theory constitute the computational theory, in Marr's sense, of language processing.

Mental models theory assumes that comprehension results in the construction of representations of situations in the real world or in an imaginary world. These models are finite and computable, and they are constructed incrementally, with the model so far acting as part of the context for interpreting the current text. Within this framework, detailed accounts have to be provided of what things are introduced into mental models by particular kinds of expression in a text, and of how references back to previously mentioned individuals are distinguished from references to those previously unmentioned. Noun phrases introduce individuals or refer to individuals that were previously mentioned or that are related (e.g., as part to whole) to previously mentioned individuals. Verbs denote events that relate individuals to one another and that are themselves related to other events. The process of mapping from information in a discourse or text to mental models that represent situations in a world is a complex one, and many of its details remain to be studied. Some models represent only part of the information in a text. Such models are, therefore, associated with a partial interpretation of the text.

CHAPTER FOUR

Linguistic approaches to anaphora

Adult native speakers have a sound working knowledge of the intricacies of their native language. Linguistics attempts to make explicit those intricacies and to give a systematic account of them. Many modern linguists follow Chomsky in assuming that the grammatical rules discovered by linguists are embodied in the minds of native speakers and used in language processing. However, it is not necessary to make this Chomskyan assumption to realise that psycholinguists are likely to produce inadequate theories if they ignore the work of linguists. A psycholinguist may be a native speaker of the language he or she is working with. But linguists would be out of business if being a native speaker gave one explicit knowledge of the complexities of one's language.

This chapter presents an overview of linguistic approaches to anaphora. It shows that anaphora is a complex phenomenon, and that a psycholinguistic theory of anaphor interpretation should not be based on a consideration of simple uses of definite pronouns, the type of anaphor most commonly studied in psychological experiments. It also shows, partly by contrast with what follows, that there are many aspects of anaphoric interpretation, particularly those that depend on the use of background knowledge, about which linguists have comparatively little to say. As well as the overview in this chapter, more detailed accounts of four particular issues in anaphor interpretation will be presented in Chapters 7 to 10.

WHAT ARE ANAPHORIC EXPRESSIONS?

The traditional view of anaphoric expressions is that they are substitutes for more complex linguistic expressions that have already occurred earlier in the text, or, occasionally, that will occur later in the text (sometimes called *cataphora*). Anaphoric expressions thus allow a conciseness of expression that direct repetition of the previous expression would avoid. Indeed, direct repetition often sounds clumsy, perhaps because it ought to signal a topic shift if it is used as an alternative to a reduced form of anaphoric expression. A definite pronoun, by contrast, would typically be used when there is no topic shift (Vonk, Hustinx, & Simons, 1992). Bosch (1983) provides a useful historical survey of the study of anaphora.

This book is primarily concerned with nominal and verbal anaphora, and not with temporal anaphora, which was discussed briefly in Chapters 2 and 3. Table 4.1 gives examples of the main types of anaphoric expressions in English. As the table shows, nominal anaphors are typically noun phrases. In particular, and despite their name, most pronouns behave syntactically as noun phrases, and have the same kinds of meaning as noun phrases (not nouns). For example, a definite pronoun such as "it" usually refers to a particular object, just as a definite noun phrase (e.g., "the balustrade") does. Pronouns can also stand for sentence meanings (sentential "it") and meanings of predicates (predicational "it").

Verbal anaphora is more complex, particularly in English. In verb phrase ellipsis, as the name suggests, a whole verb phrase is omitted, or replaced by a form of the word "do" or "be". "Do so" and "do it" are also verb phrase anaphors, but they differ in certain respects from verb phrase ellipsis. "Do it", in particular, is more restricted than verb phrase ellipsis, and cannot be used to refer to states. It also has affinities with definite pronouns, as might be expected from the fact that it includes the pronoun "it" (see Chapter 7 on deep and surface anaphora). Verb phrase ellipsis can also occur with infinitival complements, as in 4.1.

(4.1) John wants to buy a new stereo, and Bill wants to, as well.

However, the superficially similar null complement anaphora, in which the infinitival "to" also disappears, is more restricted in its occurrence—only certain verbs (e.g., "volunteer", see Table 4.1) allow null complements to follow, and like "do it" null complement anaphora has affinities with pronominal forms.

The other types of verbal anaphor shown in Table 4.1 appear, like verb phrase ellipses, to be genuine ellipses. However, they are more restricted in their occurrence. Gapping for example cannot occur across sentence boundaries, and is awkward, if not impossible, outside of sentences coordinated with "and", "or", "nor", and for some speakers "but" (Jackendoff, 1972).

TABLE 4.1
Types of anaphora in English

Name	Deep or surface	Example
definite NP anaphora	deep	A man and a woman came into the room. The man sat down.
epithet	deep	A man ran into my car. The idiot wasn't looking where he was going.
reflexive pronoun	agreement marker?	John bought himself a hamburger.
definite pronoun	deep	The guards trooped into the barracks. They took off their uniforms.
indefinite pronoun	deep	Sally admired Sue's jacket and then she got one for Christmas.
sentential "it"	deep	My aunt wants to come for Christmas. I don't believe it.
demonstrative	deep	Tom has been caught shoplifting. That boy will turn out badly.
verb phrase ellipsis	surface	I'd love to take up ski-ing and one day I'm sure I will.
noun phrase ellipsis	surface	I have read Fred's letter, but I haven't read Bob's.
sluicing (IP ellipsis)	surface	Someone has stolen my wallet but I don't know who.
gapping	surface	Mark went on a day trip to London and Fred on a long weekend to Stratford.
pseudogapping	surface	Sally suspected Joe, but she didn't Holly.
stripping	surface	Fred likes eating baked beans, but not spaghetti.
"do it" anaphora*	deep	I'd like to be able to run three miles, but I don't seem to be able to do it.
"so/not" anaphora	deep	Is John coming tonight? I think so/I think not.
null complement	deep	The team needed someone to launder their kit so I volunteered.

* Related forms include "do that" and "do the same".

WHAT DOES A LINGUISTIC ACCOUNT OF ANAPHORA TRY TO EXPLAIN?

The Chomskyan view is that a linguistic account of anaphora explains what native speakers of, for example, English know about anaphoric relations in the language that they speak. More neutrally linguistic rules can be thought of as providing a systematic description of, and ideally an explanation of, the forms that utterances take and the meanings that they have. Linguistics has many branches. The ones that are relevant to the discussion in this book are morphology, syntax, semantics, and pragmatics.

How does a linguistic account contrast with a psychological account?

A psychological account of anaphora details the mental representations and processes used in the production and interpretation of anaphoric expressions. While such an account must be sensitive to linguistic descriptions of anaphora it should also explain why people sometimes use anaphoric expressions in ways that linguistic descriptions forbid, and how such uses affect comprehension. A psychological account also addresses questions about, for example, the time course of comprehension, which linguists do not concern themselves with.

As well as differing in their goals, linguistic and psychological approaches to anaphora also differ in their methods. Chapter 5 summarises the most important methods used by psycholinguists. Linguists rely mainly on their knowledge of their native language for data about when the use of particular anaphoric expressions is appropriate. Their theories are intended to explain these data.

Morphology

Full noun phrase anaphors do not differ morphologically from other noun phrases. English pronouns form a closed lexical class, and are morphologically marked for gender (e.g., "he" versus "she"), number (e.g., "he" versus "they"), case (e.g., "he" versus "him"), and animacy (e.g., "he" and "she" versus "it"). The case of a pronoun is determined by the grammatical role it plays in its own clause (subject versus direct, indirect or prepositional object). Gender, number and animacy, on the other hand, depend on what the pronoun refers to, how that referent was introduced, or how it might normally be described. So, a male person is "he" or "him", a female person "she" or "her", and an inanimate object "it". There are inevitably complications. A person might, as an insult, be referred to as "it". There is some choice, though not wholly arbitrary, in deciding whether to use masculine and feminine or neuter pronouns to refer to animals. Some people use "he/him" or "she/her" to refer to certain inanimate objects (favoured vehicles, for example). Some objects have conventionally plural names in English (e.g., "trousers"), which they might not have in another language (e.g., French, "le pantalon", masculine singular). Others are conventionally singular in English (e.g., "hair"), but plural in other languages (e.g., Spanish, "los cabellos", masculine plural).

In addition, as these last examples show, in many languages other than English, objects are assigned arbitrary genders, which may partly or wholly coincide with the genders of names for people. Pronouns referring to those objects take the gender of the corresponding common noun. Furthermore, an object that is highly salient in its context can be referred to pronominally, even if it has not been previously referred to with a full noun phrase. In these cases, the obvious name determines the morphological form of the pronoun (Tasmowski-De Ryck & Verluyten, 1982). Thus, a parent might say 4.2 rather than 4.3 to a child playing with scissors.

(4.2)   Be careful with them!

(4.3)   Be careful with it!

And in French, one might say 4.4 to a person who is in danger of knocking over a vase ("la vase", feminine).

(4.4)   Ayez soin de ne la pas casser!
        (Be careful not to break it—FEM-SING!)

For further discussion see Bosch (1987) and Cornish (1988).

Thus, in describing the morphology of pronouns, a linguist dealing with a Western European language will have a comparatively easy job of setting out the forms and classifying them, but may have a harder job in specifying when the forms are correctly used, and how they are to be interpreted when they are so used.

Questions of morphology also arise for verbal anaphors, even when they are genuine ellipses, with no overt form in the elliptical clause. Pro-forms, with "do", carry their own morphological markings. An English verb phrase may contain any, all, or none of: a modal auxiliary, the auxiliary "have", and the auxiliary "be", in that order, and all preceding the main verb. A modal, if it occurs, forces the following verb ("have", "be", or main) to take its base, or uninflected form (e.g., "might rain", "might be raining", "might have been raining"). Similarly, "have" forces the following verb to take the past participle form, regardless of its own form ("might have rained", "has been raining") and "be" forces the following main verb to take its present participle form ("is raining", "might be raining", "might have been raining").

According to the standard verb plus verb phrase analysis of these structures, each string from the right in a string of auxiliaries followed by a main verb is a verb phrase ("raining", "been raining", "have been raining", "might have been raining") and can undergo verb phrase ellipsis if the appropriate conditions are fulfilled. Furthermore, if an auxiliary "do" appears, either in verb phrase ellipsis as it can in most British English dialects, or in a proform ("do so", "do it"), it must take the appropriate morphological form, as in 4.5–4.8.

(4.5)   John might have been eating an avocado, and Bill might have been doing so, too.

(4.6)   John might have eaten an avocado, and Bill might have done so, too.

(4.7)   John might eat an avocado, and Bill might do so, too.

(4.8)   John eats an avocado, and Bill does so, too.

In these examples, the first clause and the anaphor-containing clause have the same sequence of auxiliaries and main verb (or pro-form). Thus they describe events with similar temporal properties and temporal relations to the time of utterance. It is possible to break this semantic parallelism, though some cases are more felicitous than others, perhaps for reasons of plausibility. However, when the parallelism is broken the pro-form takes the morphological form appropriate to its own clause, as in 4.9 and 4.10.

(4.9)   John ate an avocado, and Bill might do so, too.

(4.10)   John has already eaten an avocado, and Bill is doing so, now.

Similarly, with verb phrase ellipsis, the sequence of auxiliaries before the ellipsis, and not the morphological form of the antecedent verb phrase, determines the (implicit) morphological form of the missing material, and hence the interpretation of its temporal properties, as in 4.11.

(4.11)   John ate an avocado, and Bill might eat an avocado (NOT ate an avocado).

Syntax

Syntactically, definite pronouns are noun phrases, indefinites can be noun phrases or nominals, "do it", "do so" and elliptical verb phrases are verb phrases, gaps are verbs, and so on. Some of the less common verbal ellipses, such as gapping, are confined to single sentences, so it may be appropriate to look for syntactic rules for complex sentences that allow a full first clause to be followed by, for example, a second clause containing a gap. A rule of interpretation would also be required to assign a meaning to the second clause, from the meaning of the first.

Pronouns and the various types of verb phrase anaphora are discourse phenomena that can cross sentence boundaries, as in 4.12 and 4.13.

(4.12)   John left the cinema early. He hated the film.

(4.13)   John complained to the manager about the film. Sarah did so, too.

Thus, syntactic rules need only specify where such anaphors can occur (in noun phrase or verb phrase positions), and leave questions of interpretation to discourse semantics. However, when an anaphor and its antecedent occur in the same sentence there are restrictions, which may be syntactic in nature, on how the two can be related. These restrictions are discussed later in this chapter.

One controversial question about the syntax of anaphoric expressions is whether ellipses are proforms. Paradigm examples of proforms include definite and indefinite pronouns, "do so" and "do it". If ellipses are proforms they are *null* proforms. Proforms may have their own structure (the relation between the "do" and the "so" in "do so", for example), but they do not take on the structure of their antecedents. Alternatively an ellipsis may be an empty category, but one in which the structure of the antecedent material is inherent. One example of this approach to ellipsis is found in Hankamer and Sag's (1976) theory of deep and surface anaphor, which is described in more detail in Chapter 7. Johnson (1996) refers to Hankamer and Sag's approach to ellipsis, and similar ones, as derivational. Derivational approaches can either postulate deletion of a full VP to produce the ellipsis, as Sag (1976) originally did, or reconstruction of an antecedent VP in the position of the ellipsis (e.g., Williams, 1977). In either case, the ellided VP has the same internal structure as its antecedent.

As Johnson notes, many facts about VP ellipsis suggest that the internal structure of the ellided VP determines its properties, and these facts have been used by Sag and others to argue for a derivational account. Furthermore, if derivations involve movement rules, this account can explain certain types of non-parallelism between ellipsis and antecedent, which Hankamer and Sag initially disallowed. However, there are other phenomena that appear to favour a proform account, of the kind proposed by, for example, Hardt (1993). These phenomena relate to different cases of non-parallelism, where no independently motivated movement rules can explain how the ellipsis is interpreted, as for example in 4.14, from Webber (1979).

(4.14)   China is a country that Joe wants to visit, and he will too if he gets enough money.

An attempt to save derivational accounts for these cases appeals to an extension of the process that interprets indexicals, such as "I" and "you", when ellipses cross speaker boundaries, as in 4.15.

(4.15a)   Speaker A: Come to my place tonight.
(4.15b)   Speaker B: OK, I will (= will come to your place tonight).

This process is called vehicle change (Fiengo & May, 1994). However, there are cases for which neither movement rules nor vehicle change provide a convincing account. Two of the most important are changes to negative polarity items and split antecedents. Negative polarity items, such as "any" only occur in negative clauses. If a positive ellipsis has a negative antecedent, polarity items must change, so the ellipsis in 4.16 means "give me some sweets" not "give me any sweets".

(4.16)   Bill didn't give me any sweets, but Fred did.

Split antecedents for verb phrase ellipses were discussed by Webber (1979) and include examples such as 4.17.

(4.17)   Bill wants to sail around the world and Fred wants to trek the Himalayas but neither of them can afford to.

Although Johnson (1996) favours a derivational approach to VP ellipsis, he concedes that no fully adequate account of this kind has yet been produced. He also points out that NP ellipsis and Sluicing, which is the ellipsis of a so-called Inflection Phrase (IP), appear to be similar phenomena. In addition, Pseudogapping (Levin, 1986) may be a variant of VP ellipsis. Pseudogapping is illustrated in 4.18, where the object of "eat" is present in the second clause. If Pseudogapping is a variety of VP ellipsis, "peas" must have been moved out of the VP before the deletion occurs. Johnson argues that the process most likely to have moved the object is scrambling, but he recognises that this idea is problematic, because scrambling is not a phenomenon that usually occurs in English.

(4.18)   John was eating beans and Fred was peas.

THE MEANING OF ANAPHORIC EXPRESSIONS

The traditional view of anaphoric expressions, though one that has increasing come under attack, is that such expressions are linked to other expressions in the same text, and that they take their meaning from those other expressions. More specifically, an anaphoric expression is said, according to this view, to have the same meaning as another expression in the text. The other expression, which is called the *antecedent* of the anaphor, usually, as the term suggests, precedes the anaphor. It may, however, follow the anaphoric expression, as in 4.19 and 4.20.

(4.19)   Behind him, John heard a noise.

(4.20)   If you want to, you can play in the garden.

These cases of so-called *backwards anaphora*, or cataphora, are considerably more constrained than ordinary, or forwards anaphora.

Since the term *meaning* itself has different meanings, there is more than one way in which an anaphoric expression can have the same meaning as its antecedent. Specifically, it may have the same *referent* as its antecedent or the same *sense*. These two cases have been referred to as *identity of reference* and *identity of sense* anaphora (Grinder & Postal, 1971).

Certain straightforward uses of definite pronouns ("he", "she", "it", "they") provide the paradigm cases of identity of reference anaphora in English. In a sequence such as 4.21 "he" in the second sentence refers to the same person as the proper name "John" in the first sentence.

(4.21)   John came into the room. He sat down.

Correspondingly, certain straightforward uses of indefinite pronouns ("one", "some") are paradigm cases of identity of sense anaphora. For example, in 4.22 "one" in the second sentence does not refer to the same shirt that John bought, but to another thing of the same kind.

(4.22)   John bought a new shirt. Bill bought one, too.

Likewise, most verbal anaphors produce references to events of the same kind as those described by the antecedent-containing clause. For example, in 4.23 there are two falling-over events.

(4.23)   John fell over. Bill did, too.

On this view, the interpretation of an anaphoric expression should be straightforward. Once it has been identified, its antecedent has to be located. The appropriate aspect of the meaning of the antecedent has to be computed (sense or reference, depending on whether the anaphor is an identity of sense anaphor, or an identity of reference anaphor), and assigned to the anaphor as its meaning. For identity of sense anaphors, the referent of the anaphoric expression, if there is one, may have to be computed.

Not all definite pronouns are straightforward identity of reference anaphors. By itself this fact does not present a problem for the account of anaphor interpretation that has just been sketched, as long as these pronoun uses can be distinguished from others. For example, definite pronouns within the scope of certain quantifier expressions function like bound variables in logical systems such as predicate calculus. Thus, "him" in 4.24 does not refer to a particular person.

(4.24)   Every waiter wants customers to give him large tips.

Rather, the import of 4.24 is that for any particular waiter (call him A), then 4.25 is true (Evans, 1980).

(4.25)   Waiter A wants customers to give A large tips.

And similarly for another waiter, B, 4.26 is true, and so on.

(4.26)   Waiter B wants customers to give B large tips.

Because these cases are clearly defined, they do not pose a problem. Indeed, Bosch (1983) has argued that these are not cases of anaphoric reference at all, but cases of definite pronouns acting as agreement markers. Furthermore, he argues that definite pronouns act in the same way in corresponding sentences without quantifiers, such as 4.27.

(4.27)   John wants customers to give him large tips.

Effectively, according to Bosch, the predicate in such a sentence is a complex verb such as "to want customers to give one large tips", and in English the pronoun in such complex verbs has to agree with its subject. Another way of looking at these facts (Reinhart, 1983) is to say that the complex predicate contains a variable which, when there is no overt quantifier, is bound by a lambda abstraction operator, so that 4.27, as well as 4.24, contains a bound variable.

Evans (1980) also noted the relation between sentences such as 4.27 and their quantified counterparts such as 4.24. However, he appears to claim that all anaphoric occurrences (but not deictic ones) are similar to those in 4.27, whereas Bosch believes that only some anaphoric pronouns are syntactic agreement markers.

Bosch's claim that "him" in 4.27 is not referential is implausible, since the pronoun apparently refers to John. A different approach, which attempts to unify all types of (singular) pronouns is that of *discourse representation theory* (DRT; Kamp, 1981; Kamp & Reyle, 1993). Discourse representation theory, like the theory of mental models, stresses that sentences must be interpreted in the context of the text that has preceded them. It makes use of the notion of discourse referents (Karttunen, 1976), which do not necessarily correspond in any direct way to objects in the world, but which can provide antecedents for pronouns. So singular pronouns in the scope of quantifiers as in 4.24 can be linked to discourse referents, which in this case are like logical variables that range over individuals, rather than representations of particular individuals. However, the corresponding "discourse" referent in 4.27 is John and "him" in that sentence refers to John. In DRT preceding discourse is represented in a discourse representation structure (DRS), which may itself be complex. Restrictions on the accessibility of one part of the DRS from another explain restrictions on what a pronoun can refer to. Plural pronouns are more complicated, since their (discourse) referents have not always been introduced as such into the DRS (see Kamp & Reyle, 1993, chap. 4). For example, in 4.28 "they" refers to John and Mary, who have each been introduced separately into the preceding discourse.

(4.28)   John went into town by bus. Mary went by car. They met by the town hall.

Similar problems arise in 4.29, in which "they" refers to the set of books that Bill needs.

(4.29)   Susan has found every book which Bill needs. They are on his desk.

There are other exceptions to the idea that English definite pronouns are identity of reference anaphors. However, none of the other cases is as easy to accommodate as that of bound variables. First, not all definite pronouns following quantifiers behave like bound variables. Given that such pronouns often occur in different clauses, this fact is not surprising, since quantifier scope is only defined within a single clause. Evans (1980) discussed one set of cases, such as "they" in 4.30, which he called *E-type* pronouns.

(4.30)   Few congressmen admire Kennedy, and they are very junior.

This sentence does not mean that few congressmen have both the property of admiring Kennedy and the property of being very junior, as it would if "they" were a variable bound by the quantifier "few". That interpretation would be compatible with many senior congressmen admiring Kennedy as well. Furthermore, the corresponding sentence 4.31 does not make sense, whereas a similar sentence with a bound variable interpretation (4.32) does.

(4.31)   No congressmen admire Kennedy, and they are very junior.

(4.32)   No congressmen admire Kennedy and wash their socks.

The problem that cases such as 4.31 pose for the identity of reference account is that the only plausible antecedent expression ("few congressmen") is not a referring expression, and even if it were, the definite pronoun "they" does not refer to "few congressmen", but to that small number of congressmen that admire Kennedy. As Bosch (1983) points out, this set is not referred to directly in the above sentence (cf., "The few congressmen that admire Kennedy are very junior"), but is introduced indirectly.

Bosch points out that there are a variety of cases in which the referents of definite pronouns are introduced indirectly. In these cases it is usually clear which prior expression is responsible for introducing the referent, but it is either not a referring expression, or if it is a referring expression it does not have the same referent as the definite pronoun. Cornish (1996, 1999) argues that, in general, it is necessary to distinguish between the antecedent of a pronoun, from which it takes its interpretation, and the *antecedent trigger*, which is the expression (or it may be a deictic gesture) that introduces the antecedent into a representation of the discourse. In the cases under discussion, the antecedent trigger is a linguistic expression, but it does not have the same referent as the pronoun, and it may not be a referring expression.

Bosch discusses two other cases involving quantifiers: *donkey sentences* and *examination sentences*. The original donkey sentence (Geach, 1962) is 4.33.

(4.33)   If any man owns a donkey, he beats it.

Such sentences have been seen as posing various problems for standard bound variable analyses of pronouns following quantifiers (for example, in what they say about men who own more than one donkey). They provided part of the motivation for modern theories of discourse semantics, and in particular discourse representation theory.

The pronouns in donkey sentences cannot be analysed as E-type pronouns, and neither can the pronouns in examination sentences, such as 4.34.

(4.34)   No one will be admitted to the examination unless they have registered four weeks in advance.

Another set of problem cases are the *paycheck sentences*, such as 4.35, first noted by Karttunen (1969).

(4.35)   The man who gave his paycheck to his wife was wiser than the man who gave it to his mistress.

Bosch argues that the intended referent of the pronouns in these sentences (men who own donkeys, people who will be admitted to the examination, the paycheck of the second man) are introduced indirectly (or by inference), rather than by expressions that refer directly to them. For paycheck sentences, for example, almost everyone (in the USA in 1969) had a paycheck, so the mention of one person's paycheck can suggest the existence of another person's. Bosch argues that, because people do not typically have aspidistra pots, the same kind of reference is not possible in 4.36.

(4.36)   The vicar bought his aspidistra pot from Mrs Mulroy, and Julius got it from a jumble sale.

Thus the definite pronoun in a paycheck sentence is not acting as a simple identity of sense anaphor, as an initial analysis might suggest. A similar account can be given for example 4.37, pointed out by Hirst and Brill (1980).

(4.37)   The alligator's tail fell off, but it grew back.

Inferential introduction of antecedents also occurs in some of the cases that will be examined in detail in Chapters 7 to 10, though they do not involve quantification. Indeed, Bosch himself draws a parallel between the cases he considers and reference into anaphoric islands (see Chapter 8). From a psychological point of view, an important question is whether the antecedent is introduced into the mental model by the antecedent trigger, or whether it is only when the anaphor is encountered that the antecedent trigger is used to construct the antecedent.

A further set of problems arises because of the way entities change over time. Brown and Yule (1983) point out that 4.38 has not been properly understood, if the "it" is taken to refer to the chicken as it was introduced into the discourse model by the phrase "an active, plump chicken".

(4.38)   Kill an active, plump chicken. Prepare it for the oven, cut it into four pieces and roast it with thyme for 1 hour.

SYNTACTIC CONSTRAINTS ON ANAPHORA

Earlier in this chapter the possibility of backwards anaphora, in which the anaphoric expression precedes its antecedent, was mentioned. According to Solan (1983) many languages prohibit backwards anaphora altogether. He also claims that, in Universal Grammar, such a blanket restriction is the unmarked case. However, in English, backwards anaphora is allowed under certain conditions. There have been several attempts to define the conditions under which backwards anaphora is possible. Unlike regular forwards anaphora, backwards anaphora is only permissible within the same sentence, and most attempts to define a so-called *backwards anaphora constraint* have attempted to do so syntactically (but see later). To do so it is necessary to define *command* relations that hold between nodes in a syntactic tree. The original notion of command was introduced by Langacker (1969) who stated that:

A node A "commands" another node B if (1) neither A nor B dominate the other; and (2) the S-node that most immediately dominates A also dominates B.

Langacker then proposed that pronominalisation was possible unless the anaphor both preceded and commanded its antecedent. His proposal is therefore that backwards anaphora will only be possible if the anaphoric expression is in a different clause from the antecedent. This constraint explains why co-reference between "he" and "Arthur" is not possible in 4.39 (same clause), but is in 4.40 (different clause).

(4.39)   He said Arthur was a poor dancer.

(4.40)   As soon as he spoke, Arthur knew he was wrong.

Lasnik (1976) and Reinhart (1981) pointed out that Langacker's statement of the backwards anaphora constraint was incorrect. Lasnik introduced a new notion of command (which he called *kommand*), in which S-node was replaced by S-node or NP-node, and he rephrased the backwards anaphora constraint to state the conditions under which co-reference was impossible. There are, however, problems with this approach since two expressions can co-refer for reasons other than the syntactic relation between them. As Evans (1980) points out, "he" in 4.41 could refer deictically to a person who the speaker was pointing to and who the speaker did not know, or was not sure, was Stalin.

(4.41)   He is the same height as Stalin.

A non-co-reference rule such as Lasnik's implausibly classifies this statement as ungrammatical. Evans suggests that a notion of *referential dependency* is required in the statement of constraints on anaphora. So what is ruled out in 4.41 is that "he" refers to Stalin in virtue of being referentially dependent on the occurrence of the word "Stalin" in that sentence.

Lasnik's version of the backwards anaphora constraint allows cases such as 4.42 in which "his" commands "John", because the S that most immediately dominates "his" is the main S. However, "his" does not kommand "John", because it is part of the NP "his sketch", which does not include "John".

(4.42)   Susan admired his sketch when John showed it to her.

Reinhart claimed that Lasnik's formulation of the backwards anaphora constraint was still too restrictive, because an object pronoun that is not part of an embedded sentence or a larger NP can co-refer with an NP in a subsequent clause, as in 4.43.

(4.43)   Susan admired him when John strode down the catwalk.

Reinhart replaced S-node in the original definition of command with any branching node. She called the new relation *c-command*, and claimed that the (generally) backwards nature of the constraint on anaphora was implicit in this definition, and did not need to be stated separately. Indeed, Reinhart claimed that the constraint correctly ruled out certain cases of forwards anaphora, as in 4.44.

(4.44)   Near Bill he saw a snake.

Despite some further adjustments to the definition of c-command by Reinhart, Solan (1983) argues that the c-command analysis does not work, and that a more complex analysis is necessary.

In recent versions of generative grammar (e.g., Chomsky, 1981), the general principles governing co-reference are called *binding theory*. The theory has three basic principles. The first relates to reflexive pronouns and reciprocal expressions (such as "each other"). These expressions are called, misleadingly from our point of view, anaphors. Principle A of binding theory says that such expressions must have a c-commanding antecedent in their governing category (roughly, the smallest noun phrase or clause in which they are included). Definite pronouns (called pronominals) are subject to Principle B, which states that they cannot have an antecedent in the same governing category. So anaphors and pronominals are in what is called *complementary distribution*. Where one can occur the other cannot. Principle C applies to R-expressions (referring expressions such as proper names and some full noun phrases). It states that such expressions cannot have c-commanding antecedents at all. Principles B and C both state conditions under which co-reference cannot occur, as in Lasnik's formulation of the backwards anaphora constraint (see earlier). Indeed, Chomsky follows Lasnik in treating all definite pronouns in the same way, and does not distinguish those that are bound variables (Bosch, 1983; Evans, 1980).

Chomsky (1986) presented a revised version of binding theory, following the discovery of empirical inadequacies in the earlier version. For example, both reciprocals and definite pronouns can co-refer with a subject NP, if they are possessives, as in 4.45, so the two are not in complementary distribution.

(4.45a)   The women bought each other's books.
(4.45b)   Jane bought her book

More recently it has been suggested that in languages other than English it is necessary to distinguish between (at least) two different binding domains (see, e.g., Reuland & Koster, 1991). In addition, some reflexives can be used *logophorically*, as in 4.46.

(4.46)   The chairman invited my wife and myself for a drink.

Such logophoric uses are referential ("my wife and myself" is roughly equivalent to "me and my wife") and are not subject to Principle A of binding theory.

Function/argument interpretation of the constraints

A conceptually different treatment of constraints on backwards anaphora is to describe them semantically rather than syntactically (Bach & Partee, 1980; Keenan & Faltz, 1985). On a formal semantic analysis, when expressions combine syntactically, one expression acts semantically as a function and other expressions as the arguments of that function (see Chapter 2). On this view an anaphor cannot occur as an argument of a function containing its antecedent, or vice versa. Reinhart (1983) and Bosch (1983) argue that the syntactic and semantic approaches inevitably parallel each other closely, though there are cases in which their predictions diverge, usually ones where linguistic judgements are not clear. Bosch argues that the semantic approach is better motivated, and that the constraint can be explained by what function and argument mean. However, he claims that function–argument structures are focus sensitive, with new information being treated as function and old information as argument. He also claims that, for two sentences with the same syntactic structure, co-reference may be possible in one but not in the other. For example, co-reference between "him" and "Max" is possible in 4.47, but not in 4.48.

> (4.47)   Julia hit him before Max left in his Rolls-Royce for a dinner engagement at the Ritz.

> (4.48)   Julia hit him before Max left.

However, it is possible to suggest that 4.47 and 4.48 have different syntactic structures (e.g., Reinhart, 1983), and not just different focus structures. Reinhart also rejects Lasnik's idea that the backwards anaphora constraint prohibits co-reference. Indeed, she claims that syntactic constraints on anaphora apply only to bound variable readings of pronouns. Pragmatic principles tend to ensure that pronouns that are interpreted as referring expressions are in complementary distribution to those that are interpreted as bound variables. But there are conditions under which those pragmatic principles can be violated.

DISCOURSE CONSTRAINTS ON ANAPHORA

Despite attempts to characterise pronominalisation within transformational generative grammar, and despite attempts to formulate the backwards anaphora constraint syntactically, anaphora is a discourse phenomenon. It is therefore likely that there are constraints at the discourse level on the use of anaphoric expressions. From a discourse perspective, the question about anaphora is usually phrased in the following way; what factors determine the appropriate referring expression to use at a particular point in a text (e.g., Bolinger, 1979)? Should it be, for example, a full noun phrase, a proper name, a demonstrative, a definite pronoun, or a zero form? These types of expression differ in how much semantic information they contain, and hence in how much they can contribute to the identification of an individual. An expression that has little semantic content (e.g., a definite pronoun) or even none (a zero form) can contribute little or nothing to the identification process, and can only be used where identification of the referent is either straightforward or not an issue.

A strong version of the theory that anaphoric expressions function to identify referents would predict that the least specific device compatible with the identificatory function is always used. Such a theory would be based on the idea that identification is the only role of referring expressions. However, this theory is incorrect (e.g., Bolinger, 1979; Fox, 1987; Linde, 1979). Fox studied the use of anaphoric expressions in both spoken and written English, and argued that the primary determinant of whether a pronoun was used in preference to a repeated noun phrase was whether the anaphor was in the same structural unit as the initial mention. Marslen-Wilson, Levy, and Tyler (1982) make the stronger claim that the entire history of how an entity has been referred to determines the current choice of referring expression. Fox identified several non-structural factors, for example indicating a disagreement or emphasising a contrast, that discourage the use of pronouns. Vonk et al. (1992) also argue that overspecific referential devices have a discourse structuring function. They showed experimentally both that the occurrence of such a device was taken to signal a thematic shift and that writers use such devices when asked to produce such a shift.

Fox confined her analysis to pronouns that would not be governed by the syntactic constraints discussed in this chapter. Bolinger, on the other hand, argues that there is no satisfactory formulation of the syntactic constraints, and that discourse-level factors explain co-reference possibilities even within sentences. Bolinger makes many interesting observations, some of which are similar to those that motivated Bosch's suggestion of focus-sensitive function–argument structures, and Reinhart's claim that sentences with apparently identical syntactic structures were structurally different.

SUMMARY

Linguistics has different goals from psycholinguistics. Nevertheless, psycholinguists need to know the intricacies of language, if they are to develop satisfactory theories of how it is understood and produced. To formulate theories of how anaphoric expressions are interpreted, psycholinguists must know their properties and be able to explain how they are identified and how they are assigned meanings. In English the properties of anaphoric expressions are simple, but the assignment of meaning to them is not. Furthermore, linguists are not agreed about such fundamental questions as whether within-sentence constraints on antecedent–anaphor relations, which severely restrict the possibility of backwards anaphora or cataphora, are best described syntactically, semantically, or by discourse function.

CHAPTER FIVE

Psycholinguistic approaches to anaphora: Methodological issues

This chapter briefly introduces the methodologies used in the study of anaphoric processing and discusses potential problems with those methodologies. The chapter also considers what can be learned from the use of anaphors in published texts.

EXPERIMENTAL METHODOLOGIES

Most research on the interpretation of anaphoric expressions has used the standard experimental paradigms of cognitive psychology and psycholinguistics. In particular, the most popular technique is self-paced reading, which has many variants. Other methodologies include eye-movement monitoring and "priming", as well as pencil and paper tasks, such as completing sentences or making judgements about their acceptability.

Self-paced reading

In self-paced reading experiments, people read texts by pressing a button so that parts of the text are displayed on a computer screen. Each press causes a new part of the text to be exposed and, in some versions of the paradigm, the previous portion to be deleted. The computer measures the time between the button presses, which is related, though not necessarily directly, to the time taken to read and interpret the newly displayed text.

There are many variants of this paradigm.

- The amount of new text displayed at each button push can be a word, a fixed number of words, a phrase, a clause, a sentence, or any other unit chosen by the experimenter.
- The display can be cumulative, with each button press adding more of the text to what is already displayed on the screen. Alternatively, the button presses can cause the next part of the text to *replace* what is already on the screen.
- The position of the new display relative to the old display can vary. Cumulative displays typically follow the format of normal text, either left-justified or justified at both margins, though they need not do so. Non-cumulative displays can also place text in the position it would occupy if the entire text were present, in the so-called *moving window* paradigm. The area of the screen outside the moving window may either be blank, or it may show how the words are disposed, for example by retaining spaces and punctuation, but replacing every letter by an underscore. Alternatively, non-cumulative displays may always be centred on the screen, always be left-justified on the same line, occur on lower lines of the screen, or follow whatever sequence the experimenter chooses.
- The instructions on how the text should be read (e.g., "normally", carefully) can be varied, as can the experimental task, which might be to answer one or more questions after every text, or after selected texts, to answer questions after all the texts have been presented, or to judge, for example, the acceptability of each text, or of one or more of the parts of the text as a continuation of what went before.

Self-paced reading experiments are straightforward to set up and analyse. There can be problems in interpreting the data from such experiments, though these problems are more acute when there are specific hypotheses about the exact locus in the text of particular effects, or about their time course. Most experiments on initial syntactic analysis of sentences, therefore, use eye-movement monitoring or other more fine-grained techniques. However, for exploratory studies, or studies in a field such as anaphor interpretation, in which many of the hypotheses are not temporally specific, self-paced reading experiments are a useful tool.

One non-natural aspect of the self-paced paradigm must be taken into consideration when non-cumulative displays are used. With such displays, texts cannot be read as they would be if they were printed on paper. In particular, it is not possible to look back to material in a display that is no longer on the screen. *Regressive* eye movements are not uncommon in ordinary reading (see Rayner & Pollatsek, 1989, chap. 4, for some descriptive statistics). Antecedents for anaphoric expressions frequently occur in a previous sentence or clause, and with non-cumulative displays, this antecedent clause or phrase will no longer be available for re-reading. In a self-paced reading experiment people may therefore be forced to rely on short-term memory to interpret the anaphoric expression, whereas in normal reading they have the choice of using memory or looking back.

A further problem in self-paced reading is that of *spillover* of processing of the text currently being read into the time in which the next section of text is (first) displayed. Such problems are particularly acute with small (e.g., one word) displays, because people can get into a routine of tapping the button at regular intervals, so that the relation between the time between button presses and the processing of a particular display is reduced or eliminated. These problems can to some extent be avoided by appropriate instructions and by using buttons with a light touch. Nevertheless, care is required in interpreting the results of self-paced reading experiments, particularly when effects appear later than expected.

Finally, there is some debate about the merits of asking people to make judgements (e.g., about whether the last clause of a passage makes a suitable ending) during self-paced reading, for two reasons. First, taking a combined measure of reading time plus judgement time might add noise to the data. However, there is evidence (e.g., Garnham, Oakhill, & Cruttenden, 1992) that judgement tasks can provide cleaner data than those in which people read a text and only later answer questions about it. Second, the judgement task does not reflect ordinary reading. Indeed, the task is a metalinguistic one, which may explain why it tends to give results that map more directly onto linguistic grammaticality judgements than those obtained when people are simply asked to read.

Eye-movement monitoring

The major advantage of eye-movement monitoring over self-paced reading is that text can be presented (on a computer screen) in a normal or almost normal format, and people can be asked to read the text in a normal way. The major disadvantage is that the head almost inevitably has to be restrained, for example by using a forehead rest and a bite bar. The reason is that the experimenter wishes to know where in space the eyes are looking, but the primary signal from an eye-movement monitoring device shows where the eyes are looking relative to the head. It is only if the orientation of the head in space is known that this signal can provide information about where in space the eyes are looking. Some eye-tracking devices are able to compensate for movement of the head, but not usually with enough accuracy to determine which individual character of text the eyes are looking at. If the position of the head is fixed, not only is the calculation of gaze direction in space simple, but single character accuracy can usually be obtained.

Eye-movement monitoring studies produce more complex data sets than self-paced reading studies. The raw data take different forms in different types of system, but, are typically one- or two-dimensional signals, sampled at intervals of one or a few milliseconds. Calibration measurements are then used to convert the raw data into information about the position the eyes are viewing as the text is read. Further processing converts the position data into information about the sequence of fixations and saccades produced by the reader, and then to derived measures such as time spent reading a particular part of the sentence for the first time, total time spent reading that part of the sentence, time spent until that part of the sentence is exited to the right for the first time, likelihood of a regression during the first reading of a region, total number of regressions from a region, and so on. There is considerable debate about which of these measures are more appropriate in what circumstances, and what can be learned from effects on which measures (see Rayner, Sereno, Morris, Schmauder, & Clifton, 1989 for further discussion of the use of eye-movement measures in the study of comprehension).

As mentioned earlier, eye-tracking techniques are particularly useful when hypotheses about the time course of a particular process are being tested. For example, some theories of syntactic analysis have claimed that only certain properties of sentences (e.g., their syntactic properties) guide the initial analysis of a sentence. Such hypotheses allow predictions of the effects that should be found when the eyes first pass over a particular region of a sentence, and what effects should be found only when they return to that region, presumably for reanalysis. Many of the hypotheses about anaphora interpretation are not of this form, but eye-movement monitoring studies do have their place in this research.

"Priming"

In "priming" experiments processing of a text (either reading or listening) is interrupted by the presentation of another stimulus, most commonly a visually presented word or letter string, to which a response must be made. The task is usually either to decide whether a letter string is a word (lexical decision), in which case some of the words will be related to the prior text, or to decide whether a word was present in the text so far. The term "priming" is sometimes put in scare quotes, because it implies a mechanism for the speeding of responses, and this mechanism may not be the correct one.

When people listen to spoken passages and have to respond to visually presented words, the paradigm is called *cross-modal priming*. Cross-modal priming has most commonly been used with a lexical decision task in which some of the words presented for lexical decision are semantically or associatively related to words in the spoken passages. In an alternative, purely visual, paradigm passages are presented on a computer screen, typically one word at a time, at a rate fixed by the experimenter (see Gernsbacher, 1989 for an example of a formula used to determine presentation time). Presentation is from time to time interrupted by a visual probe. This probe is distinguished from the text itself by, for example, being presented on a different part of the screen, in a different case or font, or surrounded by asterisks. In such experiments, the task has typically been to decide whether the probe has occurred in the text so far.

When priming techniques are applied to the study of anaphor interpretation, the most common procedure is to present the (name of the) referent of the pronoun (usually a proper name), or of another character in the text, in the probe word task, or a word related to a description of the referent (e.g., "nurse" following "the doctor") in the lexical decision task. "Priming" occurs if responses to that word are speeded when compared with responses to the same word or a matched word in a control condition.

McKoon and Ratcliff (1980) argued that priming techniques are superior both to cued recall techniques (which do not measure on-line processing) and self-paced reading techniques, which suffer from confounding variables (in the study of inference, where the inference and no inference conditions typically differ in what lexical items are repeated) and from spillover effects.

The major problem with this paradigm, as applied to anaphor resolution, is the interpretation of speeded responding. The responses in the experiment are to words, but anaphor interpretation, particularly that of definite pronouns (in English, "he", "she", "it", and "they") requires the identification of who or what the pronoun refers to. The fact that a word is responded to more quickly cannot be equated with the fact that its referent (or the referent of a phrase that includes it, or the referent of a phrase that includes a semantically or associatively related word) has been assigned as the referent of a preceding pronoun. Indeed, Gordon, Hendrick, and Ledoux (1998) have shown that in probe word tasks people maintain a list of words that they expect to be tested as probes. For example, if only the proper names in sentences are tested, responses are faster than if other words can be tested as well.

Which method?

Studies using different methods do not always suggest the same conclusion about how anaphoric expressions are interpreted. So-called off-line methods (e.g., pencil and paper tasks) may, for example, provide results that appear to conflict with studies that measure what happens when people are reading or listening (on-line methods). Sometimes the reason is that the initial interpretation of an expression is not the final one, and the on-line task may be sensitive to aspects of initial interpretation, whereas the off-line task reflects the final one.

More worryingly, results from different on-line tasks may suggest different conclusions. Some researchers strongly favour one type of task over others.

However, all techniques have their problems. In addition, other aspects of a study (e.g., the number and nature of the filler items, and how well they disguise the common structure of the experimental items) can affect its outcome, more or less independently of the technique used. When results conflict, it is always useful to ask how people in the studies might be performing the task they are given, and whether there is a good reason to believe that one set of results reflects more directly than another the processes of ordinary comprehension. Conclusions that are common to studies using several techniques are almost always more secure than those based on a single technique.

A CORPUS OF ANAPHORIC EXPRESSIONS

As part of our attempt to understand the processing of anaphoric expressions Jane Oakhill and I collected, over a period of years, a corpus of attested examples of "interesting" anaphors. Initially we focused on printed material, primarily because of the ease of attestation. But later the corpus grew to include spoken examples, primarily from radio and television broadcasts. One of our primary motivations for assembling the corpus was to document an increasing realisation that many naturally occurring anaphors violate the constraints on anaphor described by linguists (see Chapter 4). Furthermore, we realised that, as our linguistic sophistication increased, more of these cases came to our attention. Presumably, therefore, such cases go largely unnoticed in ordinary language comprehension and, even though they cause minor processing difficulties, they do not cause major ones.

Criteria for inclusion in the corpus

To be included in the corpus an anaphor had to come from published or publicly "broadcast" material. With published material the details of what was published were not at issue, and items that appeared to be the result of typesetting or other errors were not included. For the relatively few spoken examples, cases where mishearing was a possibility were excluded.

The main classes of example in the corpus were:

- lack of syntactic agreement between an anaphor and its antecedent, as in 5.1, taken from a supermarket leaflet

  (5.1)   Protein: These are our body's building blocks

- references into anaphoric islands (see Chapter 8), as in 5.2, taken from BBC Television News

(5.2)   Westland did dominate question time, and the very first came from . . .

- other cases in which there is no antecedent with the correct meaning, but no single word (anaphoric island) that is closely related to the referent, as in 5.3

   (5.3)   I bedded a student for a while (a female one) but dared not tell you because you would not accept its simple goodness. (Bannister, 1983, p. 52)

- violations of syntactic constraints on surface anaphors (see Chapter 7), as in 5.4

   (5.4)   Reber says there are no coherent behavioural accounts, but that is exactly what Lundin tried to do. (Foss, 1986)

- double verb phrase ellipses, as in 5.5

   (5.5)   If only we could have discovered a hole in the ozone layer, perhaps somebody would have paid attention to us. But we couldn't, and they didn't. (*Sunday Times*, 1989)

- anaphors for which the most obvious antecedent (e.g., the closest) is not the intended one, as in 5.6, where "it" means the port, not the glass

   (5.6)   Port was a pleasant contrast with the dinner. The port itself was from an excellent vintage and Macrorie had to restrain himself from gulping it so fast that his glass would be empty before it had circumnavigated the table. (Sutherland, 1987, p. 25)

- examples of "this" with no parallel linguistic antecedent, as in 5.7

   (5.7)   Puffy eyes or dark shadows look worse first thing in the morning because fluids will have collected in your eye socket while you have been in a horizontal position overnight. But this will gradually drain away during the day. (*Living Magazine*, 1988)

Conclusions suggested by the corpus

The corpus shows that many uses of anaphoric expressions fall foul of linguistic prescriptions, but do not cause overt difficulties in comprehension. It is not always possible to know whether writers and readers recognise problems with these uses. In an attempt to answer this question, Oakhill and Garnham (1992) asked people to make considered judgements about a variety of examples from the corpus, saying how well written and how comprehensible they found them. In addition they were asked to rewrite texts that they found poorly written or difficult to understand. Although there were many judgements of comprehension difficulty or bad style, they were by no means uniform. The violation of a particular constraint, for example the parallelism of form constraint for surface anaphors (see Chapter 4), produced a range of judgements (between 0 out of 12 and 10 out of 12 judgements of difficulty for different texts, and between 5 out of 12 and 12 out of 12 judgements of poor style). Oakhill and Garnham conclude that there is no straightforward relation between linguistic prescriptions about how anaphoric expressions should be used and the way they are interpreted.

Problems of interpretation

Generally speaking, attestation is not a problem with printed material. What is more difficult to ascertain is the writer's intention. Many of our examples come from journalistic material, which is often written to tight deadlines, and may not be checked as carefully as, say, the text of a textbook. We do not know if the writers would have changed their texts, if they had had more time to think about them. Nevertheless, most of the examples will have been seen by several individuals, and not have been rejected as problematic for their intended audience. Some of the work described in the following chapters attempts to answer the question of if and how anaphors like those in the corpus disrupt comprehension.

SUMMARY

The understanding of anaphoric expressions can be studied using a variety of psycholinguistic techniques. These techniques include self-paced reading, eye-movement monitoring, priming, and pencil-and-paper tasks. All these techniques have their problems, and ideally converging evidence from several of them should be obtained before a particular conclusion is accepted.

A different perspective on anaphor comprehension comes from comparing the way anaphoric expressions are used in real texts with linguistic prescriptions on how they should be used. These prescriptions are often violated, without causing apparent comprehension problems. Considered judgements sometimes agree with linguistic prescriptions, but not always.

CHAPTER SIX

Psycholinguistic approaches to anaphora: Empirical studies

This chapter provides an overview of the main areas of psychological research on anaphora, focusing primarily on topics that are not taken up in depth in the following chapters.

Garnham (1987) suggested that there are three main aspects to the interpretation of anaphoric expressions, which are a special case of expressions with context-dependent interpretations.

- The identification of anaphoric expressions in a text or discourse.
- The recognition of the aspects of linguistic and non-linguistic context that are relevant to their interpretation.
- The derivation of their meaning from their own semantic content, and the aspects of context recognised as relevant to their interpretation.

The statement of the second point is somewhat misleading, as it suggests that only when an anaphoric expression has been recognised, is an attempt made to identify relevant aspects of context. In fact, the ongoing processes of discourse comprehension change the context that is potentially relevant to the interpretation of upcoming anaphoric expressions. Indeed, this changing of context is part of a more general process whereby information from the current utterance changes the context (mental model) that is relevant to interpreting all aspects of the next utterance (Isard, 1975).

IDENTIFICATION OF ANAPHORIC EXPRESSIONS

Anaphoric expressions are not difficult to identify. Some, such as definite pronouns, belong to closed lexical classes. Occasionally there may be potential lexical ambiguities that affect the recognition of such words. The English indefinite pronoun "one", for example, is homophonic and homographic with the number name "one". The Dutch definite pronoun "zij" is ambiguous between third person feminine singular and third person plural.

The case of definite noun phrases, which in English can be recognised by the initial occurrence of a definite article or another appropriate determiner, is somewhat more complex. Not all definite noun phrases are anaphoric, but almost all have context-dependent interpretations. Those that do not are typically proper names, such as "The Golden Gate Bridge".

Elliptical verbal constructions are more complex. Some contain words from closed lexical classes, such as "do", "so", and "it", which again may be ambiguous, with main verb "do", for example, or the subordinating conjunction "so". Others genuinely elide material, as in those cases of verb phrase ellipsis that do not require a form of "do", and in constructions such as gapping, stripping, and sluicing (see Table 4.1). Generally speaking, syntactic constraints on what constitutes a well-formed sentence will allow readers and listeners to identify where such ellipses have occurred.

There has been little psycholinguistic research on how anaphoric expressions are identified, although Simner and Garnham (1999) have investigated whether an elliptical verb phrase is harder to interpret if the "do" in it could potentially be interpreted as main verb "do".

TYPES OF MEANING OF ANAPHORIC EXPRESSIONS

Once an anaphoric expression has been identified, the types of meaning it can have are fixed. Singular definite pronouns, for example, usually refer to individuals (but see Chapter 4 for other uses of definite pronouns). Indeed, a particular singular definite pronoun usually refers to the same individual that has been identified by some aspect of context, perhaps by an explicit previous reference to that individual. As was pointed out in Chapter 4, such pronouns are referred to as identity of reference anaphors. Once they have been located in a text, and the aspects of context relevant to their interpretation determined, they can be taken to refer to the individual identified by context as determining their interpretation. Identity of sense anaphors, on the other hand, such as the indefinite pronouns "one" and "some", refer to something else of the same kind as what is identified by context. For example, 6.1 does not say that I want Fred's shirt, but a shirt like Fred's.

(6.1)   Fred has a Reebok shirt and I want one, too.

Elliptical verb phrases are also identity of sense anaphors, but unlike "one" they do not refer to individuals. A few definite pronouns also appear to act as identity of sense anaphors, though they probably refer to an object indirectly introduced into a discourse model, rather than by the usual identity of sense mechanism (see the discussion of "paycheck" sentences in Chapter 4).

From a psycholinguistic point of view, the questions of what kind of meaning an anaphoric expression has, and whether it is an identity of sense or an identity of reference anaphor, are not usually addressed. However, they do affect whether a new entity must be introduced into the mental model in response to reading the anaphor, what type of entity has to be in the model if the anaphor is to be interpreted correctly, and how the entity that the anaphoric expression refers to relates to entities already in the mental model.

Psychological studies of anaphor interpretation have focused primarily on the second aspect of interpretation identified by Garnham (1987), namely how anaphoric expressions are associated with the relevant aspect of linguistic context (there have been few studies of non-linguistic context). The following section covers research on this topic, starting with the role of morphological markings on anaphoric expressions themselves, and moving up to the role of discourse-level factors.

ASSOCIATING ANAPHORIC EXPRESSIONS WITH ASPECTS OF CONTEXT

Morphosyntactic factors (gender and number)

In English, pronouns are marked for gender, number, case, and animacy. As discussed in Chapter 4, the case of a pronoun is determined by the role it plays in its own clause, whereas gender, number, and animacy are determined by what the refers to. Case does not directly affect the process of determining a pronoun's referent, though it could have an indirect effect, for example via considerations of parallel function (see later in this chapter). Gender, number, and animacy are more directly related to reference. In English it is usually difficult to determine whether the number, gender, and animacy of a pronoun are determined directly by the object or objects referred to, or whether linguistic factors play a role. However, in other languages, where names for objects have arbitrary non-semantic genders, linguistic factors are important, both when there is an explicit linguistic antecedent, and when there is not. For example, the gender of a pronoun referring to an object that is highly salient in the context is determined by the name of the object, even if the name has not been explicitly used (Bosch, 1987; Cornish, 1988; Tasmowski-De Ryck & Verluyten, 1982). There are also a few cases in English that illustrate the role of linguistic factors in determining the form of pronouns. One says "the pants ... they ..." not "the pants ... it ...", even though a pair of pants is a single object (and, indeed, one can say "a pair of pants . . . it . . ."). In other languages, cognate words may be singular (e.g., French "le pantalon").

The role of gender matching in the interpretation of pronouns has been widely studied. Ehrlich and Rayner (1983) and Matthews and Chodorow (1988) showed that a gender cue could eliminate a preference for an early as opposed to a late antecedent. Garnham, Oakhill, Ehrlich, and Carreiras (1995) showed that the effects of gender matching are no larger when gender has a semantic reflex (typically in references to people) than when it is arbitrary (in references to objects in French and Spanish). However, other studies (e.g., Garnham et al., 1992; McDonald, 1997) suggest that the use of gender matching is under strategic control, perhaps surprisingly given that it is a readily available and usually highly reliable cue at least to whether a noun phrase is a potential antecedent for a pronoun. However, as Garnham et al. (1992) point out, it is unlikely that ordinary readers would be insensitive to a flagrant gender mismatch such as the one in 6.2.

(6.2)   The manageress did not offer a refund.
He thought the customer had damaged the book.

It may simply be that when people are reading more carefully, for example because they are expecting comprehension questions, a gender cue speeds up the extra processing they perform.

Cacciari, Carreiras, and Cionini (1997) investigated the role of morpho-syntactic gender for Italian *epicenes*, nouns such as "la vittima" (the victim) which have a fixed syntactic gender (feminine in this example) but can refer to both males and females. Pronouns (Exp. 1), proper names (Exp. 2), and clitics (Exp. 3) that followed such epicenes were read more quickly if they matched the epicene in gender. Similarly a proper name before the epicene (Exp. 4) produced faster reading times when it matched the gender of the epicene. However, reading times when there was a gender mismatch were no greater than when the antecedent was a word that was not morphologically marked for gender (such as "l'erede", the heir).

Compared with gender, there have been few studies of the role of number in pronoun interpretation. Garrod and Sanford (1982) report an experiment in which singular and plural pronouns were interpreted equally easily in subject position, as in 6.3c, but plural pronouns were interpreted more easily in object position, as in 6.4c, in each case following a conjoined subject in the previous sentence.

(6.3a)   It was a fine Saturday morning.
(6.3b)   John and Mary went into town.
(6.3c)   She/they/Mary wanted some new clothes.

(6.4a)   The library was quite full.
(6.4b)   Linda and Jim could not sit down anywhere.
(6.4c)   The librarian told him/them/Jim to wait.

However, Sanford and Lockhart (1990) found a (small) preference for plural subject pronouns over singular subject pronouns in continuations of passages in which a conjoined NP was previously introduced.

Albrecht and Clifton (1998) found that plural pronouns were easier to understand than singular pronouns whether their antecedents were in subject or object position, when those antecedents were in conjoined noun phrases, though there was also an overall advantage for antecedents in subject position. In a second, eye-tracking, experiment Albrecht and Clifton (1998, Exp. 2) found that the presence of an additional possible antecedent for a singular pronoun, as in 6.5, did not increase the cost of splitting the conjoined antecedent to find an antecedent for the singular pronoun.

(6.5)   Pam and Stan asked the usherette for assistance.
        She quickly followed the usherette to the seats.

However, the locus of the splitting cost was different in 6.5 and the corresponding unambiguous case 6.6, in which it manifested itself earlier.

(6.6)   Stan and Pam asked the usherette for assistance.
        He quickly followed the usherette to the seats.

Albrecht and Clifton interpret their results as showing that readers wait to see if they need to split a conjoined noun phrase. In 6.5 they find they need to split "Pam and Stan" when they encounter "the usherette" in the second sentence. In 6.6, however, they know they need to split "Stan and Pam" on reading "he".

Gordon, Hendrick, Ledoux, and Yang (1999, Exp. 2) report a similar finding, though their explanation is that a conjunct is less prominent (see later for a detailed definition) than a conjoined NP, and hence less available as a referent of a pronoun. Gordon et al. also showed (1999, Exp. 3) that there was no first mention effect between the two conjuncts of a conjoined NP (Albrecht & Clifton had used references back to the first conjunct only). Stevenson, Nelson, and Stenning (1995, Exp. 2) also report a lack of first mention advantage in reading times for antecedents in conjoined NPs, but they do report a small (5%) advantage for eventual assignments. Further experiments (Gordon et al., 1999, Exp. 4 and 5) demonstrated similar effects for antecedents embedded within possessive NPs (e.g., "Bill's aunt") to those found for conjuncts.

Clifton and Ferreira (1987, Exp. 1) showed that a sentence containing a plural pronoun "they" was read as quickly following a sentence containing a conjoined noun phrase antecedent ("John and Mary") as when it followed a sentence containing a (syntactically) divided antecedent ("John pushed Mary"). They interpreted this result to mean that the plural pronoun found its antecedent in a discourse representation, rather than a superficial one, which should have favoured the syntactically coherent antecedent.

Carreiras (1997, Exp. 1 and 2) used a continuation task to show that plural pronouns were processed more easily when their antecedents were spatially close in the world of the text, rather than when their antecedents were conjoined NPs, a result that is consistent with Clifton and Ferreira's interpretation of their findings.

Clifton, Kennison, and Albrecht (1997, Exp. 1) studied the role of case in pronoun interpretation. "Her" is ambiguous between accusative and genitive, whereas the corresponding masculine forms, "him" and "his", are not similarly ambiguous. Off-line judgements showed that the choice between accusative and genitive readings of "her", in fragments such as "They helped her . . ." and "They burned her . . . ", were strongly affected by whether the verb preferred an animate direct object (e.g., "help", accusative reading preferred) or an inanimate direct object (e.g., "burn", genitive reading preferred). However, these effects were not reflected in on-line processing (eye tracking) measures.

Gernsbacher (1991) points out that there are cases, such as 6.7, in which a so-called *conceptual* pronoun does not agree in number with its (apparent) antecedent.

(6.7)   I think I'll order a frozen margarita. I just love them.

She identified three types of case in which such pronouns occur: multiply occurring items (as in 6.7), references to generic types, as in 6.8, and references to members of collective sets, as in 6.9.

(6.8)   My mother's always bugging me to wear a dress.
        She thinks I look good in them but I don't.

(6.9)   The substitute teacher begged the class to stop misbehaving.
        But they didn't pay any attention to her.

Gernsbacher showed that such pronouns were rated more natural and read more quickly than when the apparently illegal plural pronouns were replaced by singular pronouns ("it" in 6.7–6.9). However, in corresponding sentences that introduced unique items, specific tokens, or individual members of a set, the normal singular pronoun was preferred.

Oakhill, Garnham, Gernsbacher, and Cain (1992, Exp. 3) compared conceptual pronouns directly with non-conceptual uses of the same pronouns (typically "they" or "them"). Thus, they compared, for example, 6.10a with 6.10b.

(6.10a)   I need a plate. Where do you keep them?
(6.10b)   I need some plates. Where do you keep them?

They found that in only one of Gernsbacher's three cases, that of collectives, was the conceptual pronoun understood more rapidly than the plural reference to the explicit plural antecedent.

Syntactic factors

Matthews and Chodorow (1988) compared pronouns with early (6.11a and 6.12a) and late (6.11b and 6.12b) antecedents. They also considered the effect of more (6.11b) or less (6.12b) deep embedding of the antecedent.

(6.11a)   After the bartender served the patron's drink, he got a big tip.
(6.11b)   After the bartender served the patron's drink, he left a big tip.

(6.12a)   After the bartender served the patron, he got a big tip.
(6.12b)   After the bartender served the patron, he left a big tip.

They suggest that in the absence of a gender cue people perform a left-to-right, top-down, breadth-first search within the current sentence in an attempt to find an appropriate antecedent (as suggested by Hobbs, 1978).

As mentioned in Chapter 4, linguists have attempted to describe conditions under which two expressions in the same sentence can be co-referential. Such conditions make use of one or other of the command relations between nodes in syntactic trees, most usually Reinhart's (1981) notion of c-command, repeated here for convenience.

Node A c-commands node B if and only if the first branching node above A in the tree dominates B.

Cowart and Cairns (1987, Exp. 1) showed that the occurrence of the pronoun "they" in prior context influenced the interpretation of an ambiguous noun phrase such as "flying kites". Time to initiate the pronunciation of "is" following 6.13a was slowed compared with 6.13b.

(6.13a)   As they glide gracefully over the city, flying kites . . .
(6.13b)   If you know how to handle sudden gusts of wind, flying kites . . .

This effect was eliminated by syntactic (c-command) constraints on the reference of the pronoun (6.14a versus 6.14b) but not by selectional restrictions (6.14c versus 6.14d) or by more general pragmatic considerations (6.14e versus 6.14f).

(6.14a)   If they want to save money, visiting uncles . . .
(6.14b)   If they want to believe that visiting uncles . . .
(6.14c)   Even though they use very little oil, frying eggs . . .
(6.14d)   Even though they eat very little oil, frying eggs . . .
(6.14e)   Whenever they smile during the procedure, charming babies . . .
(6.14f)   Whenever they lecture during the procedure, charming babies . . .

Nicol and Swinney (1989) presented sentences such as 6.15 and 6.16.

(6.15)   The boxer told the skier that the doctor for the team would blame himself for the recent injury.

(6.16)   The boxer told the skier that the doctor for the team would blame him for the recent injury.

In 6.15 "himself" can only be the doctor, according to principle A of binding theory (see Chapter 4), whereas in 6.16 "him" could be the boxer or the skier. Associates of "boxer", "skier", and "doctor" were presented immediately after the anaphors in a cross-modal priming paradigm. Significant priming was obtained for just those words that named possible antecedents according to principles A and B of binding theory.

Gordon and Hendrick (1997) collected ratings from people naive to linguistic theory on the acceptability of co-reference between pronouns and proper names in a variety of syntactic configurations. A name (antecedent) followed by a pronoun (anaphor) was always highly acceptable, regardless of the syntactic configuration (c-command relation between antecedent and anaphor or not), which is as expected since the anaphor never c-commanded the antecedent within its governing category. Name–name sequences received low acceptability judgements, though there was some effect of c-command, with more positive judgements when there was no c-command relation between the two occurrences of the name. Although people were asked to say whether the two expressions could be co-referential, their judgements may have been influenced by the pragmatic oddity of repeating the name sentences such as 6.17a and 6.17b.

(6.17a)   John met John's roommates at the restaurant.
(6.17b)   John's roommates met John at the restaurant.

Pronoun–name sequences based on these sentences received low acceptability ratings, even when the pronoun did not c-command the name. Indeed there was little difference between cases in which it did, such as 6.18a, and cases in which it did not, such as 6.18b.

(6.18a)   He met John's roommates at the restaurant.
(6.18b)   His roommates met John at the restaurant.

Even in the simpler sentence 6.19, Gordon and Hendrick (1997, Exp. 3) found that only 33% of judgements were positive.

(6.19)   Her father respects Joan.

However, in other types of structure, backwards anaphora is readily accepted. For example, in Gordon and Hendrick (1997, Exp. 2), 6.20a received 88% positive ratings, whereas 6.20b received only 4%.

(6.20a)   Before she began to sing, Susan stood up.
(6.20b)   She stood up before Susan began to sing.

In further experiments, Gordon and Hendrick report three additional findings. First, acceptability judgements for co-reference depended on the mix of sentences included in the experiment (Exp. 6), a finding that, as they point out, will not be surprising to psychologists. Second, an appropriate sentential context, a question, did not affect judgements (Exp. 5). Third, NPs in what they call *prominent* positions (such as sentential subject) favoured later pronominal reference and disfavoured repeated noun reference. This finding is reminiscent of the repeated name penalty that Gordon and colleagues reported for inter-sentential anaphora (see later). In their Experiment 4, they also showed that c-command relations had a greater effect on judgements when people were asked to reflect more before responding. A later study (Gordon & Hendrick, 1999) showed that definite noun phrases and quantified expressions showed a similar pattern of judgements to proper names.

Gordon and Hendrick's general conclusion is that Principles A and B of binding theory provide a good description of linguistically naive judgements about co-reference, but Principle C does not. Thus, people recognise that there are syntactic positions where co-reference must be achieved by a reflexive or reciprocal, and that an ordinary definite pronoun in the same position cannot be co-referential with the same antecedent noun phrase. However, they argue that, outside this domain, c-command does not play the role that linguists have claimed, and suggest that its apparent effects arise because c-commanding is correlated with being prominent, which they equate with being high in syntactic structure, and not embedded in substructures. They claim that prominence is the primary factor that determines what type of referential expression is appropriate for a second reference to an individual, though it is a notion that is hard to define in a satisfactory way. Gordon and Hendrick (1998) suggest the following definition, using a modified version of Reinhart's notion of c-command, which they call n-command.

> A n-commands B if there is some node C that dominates A and B and there are n branching nodes that are dominated by C that dominate A.

Prominence is then defined using the notion of n-command.

> A is more prominent than B if A x-commands B and B y-commands A and $x < y$.

An earlier study by Hirst and Brill (1980, Exp. 2) examined the interaction of syntactic and other factors in pronoun comprehension. In 6.21 "he" and "Henry" cannot be co-referential.

(6.21)   He ran for a doctor after Henry fell down some stairs.

Nevertheless, Hirst and Brill found that the time to resolve the pronoun depends on the relative probability that the predicate "ran for a doctor" might apply to Henry or another person introduced in the context, given that Henry had fallen down some stairs, suggesting that the syntactically forbidden antecedent is considered.

Clifton et al. (1997, Exp. 2) studied the interpretation of accusative ("him") versus genitive ("his") pronouns in sentences such as 6.22a–6.22d.

(6.22a)   The supervisors paid him yesterday to finish typing the manuscript.

(6.22b)   The supervisor paid him yesterday to finish typing the manuscript.

(6.22c)   The supervisors paid his assistant to finish typing the manuscript.

(6.22d)   The supervisor paid his assistant to finish typing the manuscript.

In 6.22a and 6.22b Principle B of binding theory prevents "him" from being co-referential with the subject noun phrase, whereas it does not rule out co-reference in 6.22c and 6.22d. Number rules out co-reference in 6.22a and 6.22c. Clifton et al. found that number had an effect in the reading of 6.22c and 6.22d, suggesting that co-reference with the subject noun phrase was being considered, whereas it had no effect in 6.22a and 6.22b.

Sentence-based factors

An important experimental result within Gernsbacher's (1990) structure building framework is the advantage of *first mention* (Gernsbacher & Hargreaves, 1988, 1992). Gernsbacher and colleagues link this effect with the process of laying a foundation for the representation of the information in the upcoming sentence. According to Gernsbacher and Hargreaves the advantage of first mention is found regardless of the syntactic and semantic role played by a referring expression. In particular, the effect is not specifically associated with sentential subjects, which come first in simple active sentences with no fronted constituents. It has, however, often been suggested (e.g., Crawley, Stevenson, & Kleinman, 1990; Frederiksen, 1981) that pronouns in one clause prefer to refer to the subject of the previous clause, and this preference is often hard to distinguish from a preference for first-mentioned antecedents. A preference for pronoun antecedents in subject position has been built into many computer systems for understanding natural language, back to Winograd's (1972) SHRDLU.

The advantage of first mention is usually measured using a probe word task, in which, for example, responses to Ann are faster than responses to Pam in 6.23.

(6.23)   Ann predicted that Pam would lose the track race, but she came in first very easily.

This effect was noted by Corbett and Chang (1983), whose primary object was to determine whether both potential antecedents were activated during comprehension, or whether attention could be focused on just the actual antecedent. Corbett and Chang presented probe words only at the end of sentences. In Gernsbacher's experiments other probe positions were used, in an attempt to examine the time course of the effect.

By carrying out large-scale studies, Gernsbacher was able to detect effects that had been difficult to find in earlier work. Shillcock (1982) and Tyler and Marslen-Wilson (1982) attempted to examine the reactivation of antecedents for pronouns using the cross-modal lexical decision task. Because pronouns typically occur close to their antecedents, potential antecedents for the pronoun were still activated to some extent before the pronoun was encountered. Tyler and Marslen-Wilson found no evidence of selective reactivation of the antecedent by the pronoun, and Shillcock with an improved design found only equivocal evidence.

Corbett and Chang also found that if a pronoun is replaced by a proper name, as in 6.24, responses are faster in the probe task, and differences between the antecedent and the non-antecedent are accentuated.

(6.24)   Ann predicted that Pam would lose the track race, but Ann came in first very easily.

Gernsbacher (1989) showed that repeated proper names produce their effects immediately, whereas the effects for definite pronouns were delayed to the end of their clauses, although pronouns had stronger effects when they could be resolved from their gender. Similar results—a delayed effect of pronouns and a stronger effect of unambiguous pronouns—were reported by MacDonald and MacWhinney (1990). Gernsbacher argues that a proper name is more specific than a pronoun and better able to reactivate an earlier co-referential expression. However, part of the reason that responses to the probe "Ann" are faster than responses to the probe "Pam" in 6.24 is because the second occurrence of the name itself is nearer the end of the sentence than the only occurrence of "Pam". This fact may explain the apparent inconsistency, pointed out by Gordon, Grosz, and Gilliom (1993), between Gernsbacher's findings and the repeated name penalty (discussed in more detail later in this chapter), which indicates a preference for pronominal reference over repeated names in some circumstances.

Gernsbacher also presents evidence that an anaphor suppresses the activation of non-antecedents to a greater extent than it enhances the activation of its antecedent. Indeed, less specific anaphors such as definite pronouns and zero anaphors do not produce discernible enhancement of the activation of their antecedents, only suppression of non-antecedents.

In language understanding in general, both within-clause incremental semantic processing (e.g., Marslen-Wilson, 1973, 1975), and end-of-clause wrap-up processes (e.g., Green, Mitchell, & Hammond, 1981; Mitchell & Green, 1978) occur. Because resolving an anaphoric reference typically links information in the current clause with information in a previous clause, it might plausibly be argued that it should be delayed to the end of the current clause. Indeed, sometimes resolution cannot be finalised until the end of the clause, because the requisite information is not available. This situation is particularly common with pronominal anaphors. For example, the referent of "she" in 6.25 and 6.26 depends on the last word of the second clause.

(6.25)   Sandra lied to Elaine during the trial because she was gullible.

(6.26)   Sandra lied to Elaine during the trial because she was scared.

Nevertheless, anaphor resolution can always be initiated when the anaphor is first encountered, and it can often be completed quickly as well.

Two lines of evidence support the conclusion that these processes are rapidly completed for noun phrase anaphors, consistent with Gernsbacher's claims. First, Garrod and Sanford (1985) showed that spelling errors in verbs following a co-referential proper name or definite noun phrase (e.g., "jimped" for "jumped") were more quickly detected if the action denoted by the verb was predictable, given the character's role in the scenario. The fact that the spelling errors were detected with little or no delay suggested that the anaphoric references had been resolved immediately, since the passages were written so that the consistency or otherwise of the action would not be apparent if those references had not been resolved. However, in this study, the co-referential proper names or descriptions were simply repetitions of earlier expressions in the same passage (e.g., ". . . the lifeguard . . . the lifeguard . . ." or ". . . Elizabeth . . . Elizabeth"), and inferences were not required to establish co-reference.

The second line of evidence comes from priming studies, and in particular those of Dell, McKoon, and Ratcliff (1983). In Dell et al.'s experiments, an anaphoric definite noun phrase such as "the criminal" not only immediately primed its (more specific) antecedent, "the burglar", it also immediately primed other words from the same sentence as the antecedent. Priming of "burglar" by "criminal", and hence of words close to "burglar" in the text, does not necessarily prove that co-reference has been established (see Garnham, 1994). However, O'Brien, Duffy, and Myers (1986) showed that priming was reduced in similar passages in which the relation between "criminal" and "burglar" was not anaphoric. As in Garrod and Sanford's study, little or no inferential processing was required to resolve the anaphors in O'Brien et al.'s experiment. If the link between "criminal" and "burglar" is an inferential one, it depends on a particularly simple type of inferential link, a definitional one. If a person is a burglar, they are also a criminal, and a reference to them as "the criminal", in a passage with no other criminals in it should be readily resolved.

Stylistic factors

Style manuals often recommend parallelism of various kinds. For example, they claim it is preferable to conjoin two active clauses or two passives rather than an active and a passive. It is also possible to argue for parallelism between an anaphor and its antecedent, most usually parallelism between the roles that the two play in their respective clauses.

Sheldon (1974) suggested that many of the mistakes that 4- and 5-year old children make in the interpretation of relative clauses could be explained by the hypothesis that they prefer the head noun of the relative clause to play the same role (subject or object) in the main clause and the relative clause. She also reports (Sheldon, 1977) some evidence of the use of a parallel function strategy in adults, but not to the same extent as in children. Sheldon (1974) also suggests that parallel function may play a role in adults' interpretation of pronouns.

Grober, Beardsley, and Caramazza (1978) showed that in completing sentences of the form "NP1 aux V NP2 because/but Pronoun . . .", for example 6.27, people preferred to take the pronoun to refer to NP1, rather than NP2, though this effect was modulated by other factors such as what auxiliary verb was used, the implicit causality of the main verb (see Chapter 9), and whether the conjunction was "because" or "but".

(6.27)   John may have scolded Bill because he . . .

Grober et al. interpreted these results as support for the use of parallel function—taking the anaphor to play the same role in its clause as the antecedent in its clause—in the interpretation of pronouns. However, because of the form of the fragments they used, they could not distinguish between a preference for parallel function and a preference for antecedents in subject position. The same criticism can be levelled at Crawley et al. (1990), who argue for a preference for subject antecedents. Because they used only pronouns in non-subject positions, they were not able to assess the contribution of parallel function to their results. Cowan (1980) provided further evidence for the use of parallel function, but suggested that it could be entirely overridden by real world knowledge, and modulated by other factors such as the syntactic form of the antecedent-containing clause (e.g., active versus direct object passivised versus indirect object passivised).

Smyth (1992, 1994) demonstrated parallelism effects for both subject and object pronouns. He showed (1994) that close syntactic parallelism enhances the effect, and that shared thematic roles do so, too (1992).

Stevenson et al. (1995, Exp. 1) also showed that with strict parallelism both subject and object pronouns preferentially took parallel antecedents. However, subjects showed a stronger preference for parallelism than objects (80% vs 60%). Stevenson et al., therefore, argued that the subject assignment strategy and the parallel function strategy were working together in these cases, whereas with non-subject pronouns the two strategies were in conflict, and parallel function was more important. With non-parallel predicates, subject assignment became the prominent strategy. There were 57% subject assignments for non-subject pronouns. In a further experiment Stevenson et al. (1995, Exp. 2) sought evidence for a third, parallel order, strategy, which Cowan (1980) had suggested and dismissed, but that they had previously suggested might be used (Stevenson, Nelson, & Stenning, 1993). This strategy predicts that a (non-conjoined) subject pronoun should be assigned to the first element of a conjoined subject antecedent and a non-subject pronoun should preferentially be assigned to a second conjunct. No evidence for this pattern of assignment was found.

In their second experiment Stevenson et al. (1995) also showed that the parallel function strategy contributed more to pronoun interpretation when sentences were presented out of context. They suggest that, in context, the subject assignment strategy is enhanced by a preference for continued reference to topics, which are usually realised as grammatical subjects. More generally, they claim that *heuristic* strategies, such as parallel function and subject assignment, are only important in determining the final interpretation of a pronoun when other cues, such as gender matching, or pragmatic cues based on real world knowledge, are not available.

Matching anaphor to antecedent

As mentioned earlier, morphological markings of number and gender may help to determine the reference of pronouns. Other types of anaphor may also match their antecedent. For example, proper names can be repeated, though there is some controversy over whether the greater overlap between "John" and "John" than between "he" and "John" makes "John" an easier anaphor to process (see earlier). Noun phrase anaphors can also directly repeat their antecedents (e.g., ". . . the man . . . the man . . .") though they can be related to their antecedents in other ways.

Garrod and Sanford (1977) showed that if anaphor and antecedent were related as category to instance, as in 6.28, the sentence containing the anaphor was read more quickly than when the anaphor was more specific than the antecedent, as in 6.29.

(6.28a)   A robin would sometimes wander into the house.
(6.28b)   The bird was attracted by the larder.

(6.29a)   A bird would sometimes wander into the house.
(6.29b)   The robin was attracted by the larder.

Furthermore, 6.28b was read more slowly if "robin" was replaced by a less common exemplar of the category "bird", such as "goose".

In a later experiment, Sanford and Garrod (1980) also included passages in which the antecedent–anaphor relation was category–category (". . . bird . . . bird . . .") and instance–instance (". . . robin . . . robin . . . "). They found that the reading time for the second sentence in these passages depended on the specificity of the noun in the first passage, but only when the anaphoric noun phrase was in subject position. They proposed that new information is more easily accommodated into more specific scenarios.

Garnham (1981, 1984, 1989b) reports a series of experiments with results that conflict with those of Sanford and Garrod (1980). Garnham found that the sentence containing an anaphoric reference was harder to understand when it contained extra information about the referent (e.g., ". . . bird . . . robin . . .") than in the other three cases. Garnham was unable to resolve the difference between the two sets of results, but he was able to show that his pattern of results was largely confined to people who read more slowly in the experiments, which suggested that strategic processing could be a factor.

In a further study Garnham, Oakhill, and Cain (1997, Exp. 2) showed that the problem with the "... bird ... robin ..." passages was not the presence of extra information *per se*, but the unexpected presence of that information in the anaphoric noun phrase. Following Garnham (1984), Garnham et al. made the noun phrase more specific by adding an adjective. They showed that including the adjective in the anaphoric noun phrase, as in 6.30, slowed people down compared with putting the same information in the predicate, as in 6.31.

(6.30a)   The woman looked around the jewellery shop.
(6.30b)   The rich woman bought a diamond ring.

(6.31a)   The woman looked around the jewellery shop.
(6.31b)   The woman was rich and bought a diamond ring.

McKoon and Ratcliff (1980) studied passages with noun phrase anaphors that either repeated the head noun of the antecedent ("... a burglar ... the burglar ...") or replaced it with a corresponding category noun ("... a burglar ... the criminal ..."). They found that both types of anaphor speeded responses to "burglar" re-presented as a probe word. Furthermore, they also speeded responses to other words in the same sentence as the original occurrence of "burglar". A follow-up study by Dell et al. (1983), mentioned earlier, showed that activation of the antecedent word ("burglar") and other words from the initial sentence occurred as soon as 250 ms after the anaphor was read. The antecedent word remained activated until the end of its sentence, but activation of other words from the earlier sentence died away. O'Brien et al. (1986) provided a further set of controls for this study, and replicated Dell et al.'s basic reinstatement effect.

Greene, Gerrig, McKoon, and Ratcliff (1994) examined the processing of *unheralded pronouns*. Gerrig (1986) defined unheralded pronouns as pronouns whose referents cannot be found in the immediate discourse environment. Some such pronouns have no linguistic antecedents at all, but the ones studied by Greene et al. have no immediate antecedents. According to Greene et al. such pronouns will be readily understood when common knowledge between the speaker or writer and their audience puts the referent of the pronoun in the focus of attention. They used passages in which a subsidiary character mentioned only briefly at the beginning was associated with one of the main characters in the passage (e.g., as a cousin or a mugger). The middle of the passage focused either on the main character associated with the subsidiary character, or the other main character. After this middle episode the briefly mentioned character was more accessible in the first case, and less accessible in the second. However, the use of a (locally) unheralded pronoun at the end of the passage made that character highly accessible again.

McKoon, Gerrig, and Greene (1996) showed that the unheralded pronouns activated other concepts related to their referents, just as noun phrase anaphors had done in McKoon and Ratcliff's (1980) and Dell, et al.'s (1983) studies. They also found that the effects they report did not depend on the presence of an anaphoric reference. According to McKoon et al. (1996) the results support what they call a *memory-based* account of text processing. On this view information about features of the current part of a text spreads, passively and in parallel, through long-term memory and *resonates* with matching information. Although the information might in principle spread to all of long-term memory, in practice the spreading signal quickly weakens to the point where it cannot produce discernible resonance. Unheralded pronouns are possible because the information spreads to all of long-term memory, not just the part that contains a representation of the text. However, such pronouns will only successfully refer if there is a single obvious referent, determined, for example, by how the text has temporarily reorganised (or redistributed activation in) long-term memory. Since the reorganisation is independent of the occurrence of the pronoun itself, similar results are found even without the pronoun. However, this idea comes dangerously close to saying that what is being studied here is not anaphor resolution.

An unheralded pronoun may have no explicit antecedent, and the same is true of some full noun phrase anaphors, for which the antecedent must be constructed inferentially. The classic study of such *bridging inferences* in anaphor interpretation is that of Haviland and Clark (1974). Haviland and Clark showed that the second sentence in 6.32, where the referent of "the beer" has been specifically mentioned in the first sentence, was read more quickly than the second sentence in 6.33, in which it has not.

(6.32a)   We got some beer out of the trunk.
(6.32b)   The beer was warm.

(6.33a)   We checked the picnic supplies.
(6.33b)   The beer was warm.

However, Garrod and Sanford (1981) showed that such inferences do not necessarily take time. The second sentence in 6.35 was read just as quickly as the second sentence in 6.34.

(6.34a)   Mary put the clothes on the baby.
(6.34b)   The clothes were made of pink wool.

(6.35a)   Mary dressed the baby.

(6.35b)   The clothes were made of pink wool.

Garrod and Sanford (1994) suggest that the difference between Haviland and Clark's (1974) results and their own (1981) can be explained by the ease with which the anaphor maps onto the discourse representation. Dressing strongly implies clothes in a way that picnic supplies do not strongly imply beer (but see Cornish, 1999; pp. 214–218 for further discussion).

This issue was investigated further by O'Brien, Shank, Myers, and Rayner (1988; and see also Garrod, O'Brien, Morris, & Rayner, 1990 for a clarification and refinement of O'Brien et al.'s results). O'Brien et al. studied instance-to-category anaphoric links and immediacy of processing, using eye-movement monitoring. The anaphoric noun phrases (such as "the knife") were instances and the antecedents were either those same instances, or the corresponding categories (e.g., "the weapon"). O'Brien et al.'s principal concern was to show that an elaborative (forward) inference (e.g., that the weapon was a knife) could occur. They found no difference between their "knife–knife" and "weapon–knife" passages when there was a strongly suggestive context such as 6.36 (Exp. 1) or a prompt to draw an inference (Exp. 2).

(6.36)   He stabbed her with his knife/weapon.

However, with a less specific context, such as 6.37, readers spent more time reading a specific noun phrase anaphor (e.g., "the knife") when it followed a more general antecedent (e.g., "his weapon") than when the antecedent was the more specific noun phrase (e.g., "his knife").

(6.37)   He assaulted her with his knife/weapon.

This last result suggests two things. First, in the less specific context, the inference that the weapon is a knife is not made elaboratively, but is drawn in a backwards direction. Second, the inference is drawn when the anaphoric noun phrase is read. However, these conclusions must be treated with caution, since the difference between the gaze durations on the crucial noun (e.g., "knife") in the two conditions was only 20–30 ms. This difference is about one tenth that usually associated with the completion of backwards inferences. For example, Garrod and Sanford (1977, Exp. 1) found a 228 ms difference between the instance–category (e.g., "robin–bird") and category–instance (e.g., "bird–robin") conditions, and Garnham (1981), who made the same category–instance versus instance–instance comparison as O'Brien et al., also found a 228 ms difference when the context did not constrain the interpretation of the category. Therefore, although O'Brien et al.'s results suggest that early inference-based processes are initiated as the anaphoric noun phrase is read, it is likely, despite O'Brien et al.'s failure to find effects on the immediately following fixation, that most inferential processing is delayed until the rest of the sentence is read.

A result similar to that of Garrod and Sanford (1981) was reported by Walker and Yekovitch (1987). They compared definite noun phrase anaphors in subject position in three types of context, one in which the antecedent was explicit (and in object position, see Yekovitch, Walker, & Blackman, 1979), one in which it was implicit, but central to the current script, and one in which it was implicit, but peripheral to the current script. Walker and Yekovitch found that reading time for the sentences containing the anaphoric noun phrase were no different in the explicit and implicit (central) conditions, but slower in the implicit (peripheral) condition. This pattern of results only held if the context evoked the relevant script. These results suggest that concepts central to a script are immediately available as referents for anaphoric noun phrases, even when they have not been explicitly mentioned.

Discourse-based factors

The results of Garrod and Sanford (1981) and Walker and Yekovitch (1987) might be described in terms of what items are *focused* in a mental model. Indeed, most of the discourse-based factors that affect the interpretation of pronouns can be described under the head of focus. It is generally recognised that there are both local and global foci in text and that these foci relate to the local and global coherence of texts respectively (e.g., Grosz, Joshi, & Weinstein, 1995; Grosz & Sidner, 1986).

Before moving on to these effects, it is worth noting that linguists use the term *focus* in a different way, to refer to information that a sentence presents for the first time, in contrast to presupposed information. It is this sense of focus that is relevant to a set of studies by Yekovitch, Walker, and Blackman (1979). Those authors considered repeated noun phrase anaphors (e.g., ". . . the shark . . . the shark . . .") where each occurrence could either be focused (F) or presupposed (P). One of 6.38a–6.38d was followed by 6.38e, to produce the conditions FP, FF, PP, and PF respectively. Yekovitch et al. hypothesised that the focal information of one sentence provides the primary candidates for upcoming anaphoric references, and that such references preferentially take place from within the presupposed part of the next sentence. Thus, FP is the preferred configuration, and PF is the least preferred, as both elements, antecedent and anaphor, are in the less expected places.

(6.38a)   The lifeguard spotted the shark from a tower on the shore.
(6.38b)   On the shore, the lifeguard warned the diver about the current.
(6.38c)   From a distance, the shark noticed the movement in the water.

(6.38d)   In a cage beneath the boat, the diver photographed the eel.
(6.38e)   The shark attacked the diver near the reef.

The reading time for 6.38e was fastest in the FP condition, followed by FF, PP, and PF, which supported Yekovitch et al.'s hypothesis.

Local focusing effects.   In a long text, such as a novel, many individuals may be mentioned, any of which could later be referred to by a singular definite pronoun (e.g., "it"). However, almost every occurrence of that pronoun will be readily and unambiguously interpreted as referring to a particular object. Thus, the set of possible referents for a pronoun, or more generally the set of possible interpretations for an anaphoric expression, must somehow be strictly constrained. This issue can be regarded as an issue of focus, with items currently in focus being the prime candidates for providing meaning for anaphoric expressions.

According to Grosz and Sidner (1986) discourses have a linguistic structure, which divides them into segments and defines the relations between those segments (see the discussion of coherence relations in Chapter 2). The intentions of the producer of the discourse determine the global coherence of the discourse. Within a discourse segment local coherence must also be maintained. As a discourse progresses, the participants' attentional foci change from moment to moment, in a way that determines appropriate means of referring to the things that the discourse is about, and hence appropriate uses of anaphoric expressions.

Centering theory (Grosz et al., 1995; Walker, Joshi, & Prince, 1997) is a model of how attention shifts within a discourse segment, and hence a model of local coherence and focusing. According to centering theory, each utterance has a set of forward-looking centers, which are (partially) ordered. Forward-looking centers are things likely to be referred to in later utterances. The highest-ranked forward-looking center is usually the subject of the clause, but other factors can affect the ranking of the forward-looking centers. Each utterance also has one, and only one, backward-looking center, which must be a member of the set of forward-looking centers of the previous utterance. The theory recognises three relations between the centers of consecutive utterances: continuation, retention, and shift, in that order of preference. In continuations and retentions, the second utterance has the same backward-looking center as the first. In continuations this center is, in addition, the highest-ranked forward-looking center in the first utterance. In center shifting, as the name implies, the backward-looking center of the second utterance is not the same as that of the first. More recently a further distinction has been made between smooth and rough shifts (see papers in Walker et al., 1997).

There is one rule governing pronominalisation in centering theory. If any of the forward-looking centers of the previous utterance are pronominalised, then the backward-looking center of the current utterance must be. This rule does not make the strong but implausible claim that there is only one candidate for pronominalisation at any point in a coherent discourse. It does, however, claim that the resulting discourse will be incoherent if the rule is violated. The pronominalisation rule does not forbid pronominalisation of things not mentioned in the previous utterance. Indeed, Grosz et al. (1995) explicitly mention such a possibility, although they claim it is only realised under exceptional circumstances.

The claims of centering theory have been tested in several psychological studies. Hudson, Tanenhaus, and Dell (1986) interpreted their results on the ease with which certain pronouns were understood in the centering theory framework, but did not clearly distinguish between the predictions of centering theory, and other possibilities, such as the preference for antecedents in subject position.

Some more specific claims of centering theory have been tested experimentally by Peter Gordon and colleagues. Gordon et al. (1993) provided the first demonstration of what has come to be called the *repeated name penalty*, though this effect bears some relation to one reported by Lesgold (1972), who showed that memory representations of texts containing pronouns were better integrated than those with (new) proper names or (repeated) noun phrases. Unfortunately Lesgold did not run an experiment in which the only difference between the critical sentences was whether they had a pronoun or a noun phrase anaphor with the same reference.

The repeated name penalty, which shows up as an increase in reading time, occurs when the backwards-looking center of an utterance is realised as a proper name (or a definite noun phrase) rather than a pronoun, as in 6.39. Entities referred to in an utterance, other than the backwards-looking center, do not show this repeated name penalty, though if they are referred to pronominally, the backwards-looking center must be as well, or the discourse will not be coherent. Gordon et al. found that 6.40 was read just as quickly as 6.41.

(6.39a)   Bruno was the bully of the neighbourhood.
(6.39b)   Bruno chased Tommy all the way home from school one day.
(6.39c)   Bruno watched Tommy hide behind a big tree and start to cry.
(6.39d)   Bruno yelled at Tommy so loudly that the neighbours came outside.

(6.40a)   Bruno was the bully of the neighbourhood.
(6.40b)   He chased Tommy all the way home from school one day.
(6.40c)   He watched Tommy hide behind a big tree and start to cry.
(6.40d)   He yelled at Tommy so loudly that the neighbours came outside.

(6.41a)   Bruno was the bully of the neighbourhood.
(6.41b)   He chased Tommy all the way home from school one day.
(6.41c)   He watched him hide behind a big tree and start to cry.
(6.41d)   He yelled at him so loudly that the neighbours came outside.

Gordon et al. also showed (1993, Exps. 2a, 2b, and 3) that the repeated name penalty was confined to syntactic subjects, or at least it was not found for fronted constituents, such as those at the beginning of 6.42a and 6.42b.

(6.42a)   In Lisa's opinion, the painting captured Joe's mood exactly.
(6.42b)   In her opinion, the painting captured Joe's mood exactly.

A further experiment (1993, Exp. 4) showed that the repeated name penalty was much reduced after a shift of centre.

These results were extended by Gordon and Chan (1995) who showed that the repeated name penalty was associated with the grammatical subject of both active and passive sentences (Exp. 1) but not with the agent of a passive sentence, so that the thematic role of the subject, which is different in actives and passives, but the same for active and passive agents, was unimportant in determining whether the penalty occurred. They also showed (Exp. 4) that if the grammatical subject of a sentence introduces a new entity, the repeated name penalty is associated with the direct object of the sentence, because the direct object's referent and not that of the subject is the backward-looking centre. Kennison and Gordon (1997) corroborated some of these findings using eye-tracking methodology.

Gordon and Scearce (1995) considered the interaction between centering information and general world knowledge that may determine the final interpretation of a pronoun. They presented (Exp. 1) passages such as 6.43, with either 6.43c or 6.43d omitted. 6.43c provides a continuation of the discourse centre, whereas 6.43d produces a shift.

(6.43a)   Bill wanted John to look over some important papers.
(6.43b)   He had to mail him the documents by Monday.
(6.43c)   Unfortunately he/Bill never sent the papers.
(6.43d)   Unfortunately he/John never received the papers.
(6.43e)   As a result the whole deal fell behind schedule.

The reading time for the second half of 6.43d was elevated when the anaphor was a pronoun, but no such effect was found when the anaphor was a proper name. These results suggest that the pronoun is preferentially interpreted as continuing the center, and when later information shows this not to be the case, additional processing is required. In a second experiment Gordon and Scearce showed that even when the disambiguating information occurred before the pronoun, as in 6.44a and 6.44b (which replaced 6.43c and 6.43d in the previous passage), similar effects were found.

    (6.44a)   After sending the papers he/Bill began more work.
    (6.44b)   After receiving the papers he/John began more work.

Some theorists (e.g., Greene, McKoon, & Ratcliff, 1992) have made a stronger claim about definite pronouns than the one made in the latest versions of centering theory. They have suggested that at any point in a well-written discourse there is just one entity that a pronoun can refer to. As discussed earlier, centering theory make the weaker claim that if any entity referred to in an utterance is pronominalised, the backward-looking center must be. Greene et al. support their claim with data from a series of experiments in which people appeared not to resolve pronouns when they had more than one possible antecedent. However, it has been suggested that Greene et al.'s results are the result of a methodological artefact (e.g., Gordon & Scearce, 1995), because the experimental task discouraged people from engaging in normal comprehension.

It is also hard to reconcile Greene et al.'s claim with findings that pronouns that have more than one possible antecedent are harder to understand than those that have only one. Frederiksen (1981) reported an effect of this kind in an experiment in which people had to name the referent of a pronoun. Garnham (1989b, Exp. 3) reported a similar result for anaphoric noun phrases. Using the self-paced reading paradigm, he showed that people spend more time reading 6.45c following 6.45a than following 6.45b.

    (6.45a)   The knife and the rope were found beside the corpse.
    (6.45b)   The knife was found beside the corpse.
    (6.45c)   The knife had been effective.

However, Gordon et al. (1999, Exp. 1b) failed to replicate this result for proper names. People spent no longer reading the second clause of 6.46 than that of 6.47.

    (6.46)   John and Mary went to the store so that John could buy candy.

    (6.47)   John went to the store so that John could buy candy.

Chambers and Smyth (1998) extended Smyth's (1992, 1994) results on parallel function (see earlier) and used them to argue against centering theory. The preferred antecedent of an object pronoun can be the object of the preceding clause, not the subject as apparently predicted by centering theory. There was a repeated name penalty for parallel antecedents, but not for non-parallel ones (Exp. 2) and a repeated name penalty in passages such as 6.48, unless both referring expressions 6.48c were pronouns, in which case the notion of a repeated name penalty does not apply.

(6.48a)   A fight was in full swing in the back yard.
(6.48b)   Debbie punched David in the nose.
(6.48c)   Then Debbie/she slugged David/him in the ribs

However, this result was not obtained by Gordon et al. (1993), whose materials differed from those of Chambers and Smyth in several ways.

Almor (1999) argues that if the repeated name penalty arises from the failure to use a pronoun, it should also be found for non-repeated names and noun phrases (e.g., "the robin . . . the bird") in cases where, according to centering theory, the second referring expression ought to be a pronoun. He shows that the repeated name penalty does not generalise in this way, and proposes an alternative *informational load* hypothesis to explain the difficulty of interpreting anaphoric expressions. According to this hypothesis, the processing cost of a more informationally loaded anaphor must be justified either by its contribution to the identification of the antecedent or by the additional information it provides. When such an anaphor provides no additional benefit over a less informationally loaded one (such as a pronoun), it will incur a processing cost. A counterintuitive prediction from Almor's hypothesis, for which he provides experimental support, is that an anaphor that is more general than its antecedent will be easier to understand the more semantically distant it is from its antecedent if identification of the antecedent is not an issue. Thus, for focused antecedents, an inverse typicality effect is predicted with 6.49c being processed more quickly after 6.49b than after 6.49a.

(6.49a)   What the student rented was the car. (more typical vehicle)
(6.49b)   What the student rented was the boat. (less typical vehicle)
(6.49c)   The vehicle was necessary for getting to the exploration site.

Global focusing effects.   Centering theory claims that a pronoun in the current clause is likely to be interpreted as referring to the highest-ranked forward-looking centre in the previous clause. A preference for a previous subject or for the implicit cause in a preceding clause (see Chapter 9) can also be seen as a local focusing effect. In addition to these local focusing effects, there are also more global effects. For example, Anderson, Garrod, and Sanford (1983) showed that an episode shift, signalled by the elapsing of a period of time beyond which the episode would not normally continue (as in 6.50e), made an episode-bound character, such as the waiter in 6.50, less available for anaphoric reference, so that 6.50g was read slowly.

(6.50a)   The Browns were eating a meal in a restaurant.
(6.50b)   The waiter was hovering round the table.
(6.50c)   The restaurant was well known for its food.
(6.50d)   Forty minutes later the restaurant was empty.
(6.50e)   Five hours later the restaurant was empty.
(6.50f)   They had enjoyed eating all the good food.
(6.50g)   He had enjoyed serving all the good food.

Items become unavailable for anaphoric reference not just because of episode shifts, but because they become less relevant to the current discourse for other reasons. Sanford, Garrod, and colleagues have reported other character-based focusing effects. Sanford, Moar, and Garrod (1988) showed that characters introduced by a proper name are more easily referred to by a pronoun than other characters. No such difference was found for other types of anaphoric expression. More generally, Garrod and Sanford (1994) claim that pronouns are more sensitive to the focus state of their antecedents than other anaphors.

Garrod, Freudenthal, and Boyle (1994) presented passages that sometimes contained an inconsistency (e.g., a lifeguard sinking) preceded by a pronoun, repeated name or full noun phrase referring to the main or a subsidiary character, and that was either disambiguated by gender or not. With pronominal references the inconsistency was detected in initial reading, as indexed by the eye-movement record, but only when the reference was to the main character and was disambiguated by gender. More surprisingly, with the name and full noun phrase anaphors, the inconsistencies were only ever detected on re-reading.

Sanford and Garrod (1989) distinguish between anaphor resolution and a weaker relation of *bonding* between an antecedent and an anaphor. An anaphor may bond to a potential antecedent without forcing a commitment to resolution. Sanford, Garrod, Lucas, and Henderson (1984) showed that people balked when they read 6.51, though Sanford (1985a) showed that no balking occurred with 6.52.

(6.51)   Harry was sailing to Ireland. It sank without trace.

(6.52)   Harry was sailing to Ireland. It was a beautiful day.

Sanford explained this finding by suggesting that in each case the "it" bonded to Ireland, but the potential problem with the bonding only emerged if the pronoun turned out to be referential, as in 6.51, and the bonding had to be evaluated as a referential link. When the pronoun was non-referential, as in 6.52, no problems were detected.

Sanford and Garrod claim that anaphor interpretation is almost always immediately initiated, and that for full noun phrase anaphors it is also often completed immediately. For pronouns, however, completion may be delayed. This claim is consistent with Gernsbacher's results, reported earlier, but needs to be modified in the light of Garrod et al.'s (1994) findings. Those authors distinguish between the immediate primary processing of noun phrases and proper names, in which a temporary discourse referent is set up, and later secondary processing that may lead to the identification of the temporary discourse referent with a previously created discourse referent.

Many early studies of pronoun interpretation identified so-called distance effects—pronouns were read more quickly if their antecedents were near than if they were distant (e.g., Clark & Sengul, 1979; Ehrlich, 1983; Ehrlich & Rayner, 1983). Clark and Sengul suggested a backwards search for antecedents of anaphoric expressions.

Lesgold, Roth, and Curtis (1979) studied noun phrase anaphora in passages in which the material between the antecedent and the anaphor either kept the referent foregrounded, as in 6.53, or did not, as in 6.54.

(6.53a) A thick cloud of smoke hung over the forest.
(6.53b) The smoke was thick and black, and began to fill the clear sky.
(6.53c) Up ahead Carol could see a ranger directing the traffic to slow down.
(6.53d) The forest was on fire.

(6.54a) A thick cloud of smoke hung over the forest.
(6.54b) Glancing to the side, Carol could see a bee flying around the back seat.
(6.54c) Both of the kids were jumping around, but made no attempt to free the insect.
(6.54d) The forest was on fire.

The final sentence containing the anaphoric noun phrase, "the forest" was read more slowly in 6.54 than in 6.53. Furthermore, the reading time for 6.53d was not significantly faster when the intervening sentences 6.53b and 6.53c were omitted.

O'Brien (1987) pointed out that it is important to distinguish between distance effects in which the near antecedents are very near, and probably still represented in short-term memory, and those in which both (or all) possible antecedents are more distant. In a series of experiments, O'Brien (1987) showed that near (but not very near) antecedents for NP anaphors were accessed more quickly than more distant antecedents. He also showed (1987, Exp. 4) that intervening potential antecedents were reactivated when the actual antecedent was distant, but more distant ones were not, when the antecedent was near. This result is compatible with a backwards search from the anaphor through the text representation. Albrecht and Myers (1998) and

Corbett (1984) found that additional potential antecedents reduced the amount of reactivation, and O'Brien, Raney, Albrecht, and Rayner (1997) showed that when antecedents were far enough away, they were not reactivated at all.

O'Brien, Plewes, and Albrecht (1990) reported that the degree to which an antecedent was elaborated, by providing additional information about it, affected how easy it was to reinstate following an anaphoric reference. Such elaboration may take the form of additional sentences about the antecedent, but may be as little as the inclusion of a single adjective (Albrecht & Myers, 1998; see also Sanford & Garrod, 1981, p. 172). Furthermore, elaboration can cancel, or even reverse distance effects. O'Brien et al. (1990) also showed that reinstatement of potential, but not actual, antecedents depended on featural overlap between the anaphor and the potential antecedent. O'Brien, Albrecht, Hakala, and Rizzella (1995) showed that, following reinstatement, potential, but not actual, antecedents were suppressed. Misleading information may even cause an "antecedent" to be "reinstated" even if it was not mentioned in the text. O'Brien and Albrecht (1991) presented a passage in which a small animal was explicitly called a cat, but described as having a white strip down its back and producing a terrible smell. A series of experiments showed that the concept "skunk" was activated by this passage, and in one study O'Brien and Albrecht (1991, Exp. 3) the animal was frequently named as a skunk after the passage had been read.

The general pattern of O'Brien's results is consistent with Ariel's (1990) account of the accessibility of noun phrase antecedents. Ariel identifies four factors that affect the accessibility of antecedents, and hence the choice of an appropriate anaphoric expression with which to refer to them. The factors are: distance, competition (from other potential antecedents), saliency, and unity (i.e., whether anaphor and antecedent are in the same textual "unit").

Effects of clause and sentence boundaries

Wrap-up processes occur at clause boundaries (Green et al. 1981; Mitchell & Green, 1978). It would not be surprising if these processes affected the interpretation of anaphoric expressions in later clauses. Clark and Sengul (1979, Exp. 1) showed that both definite pronouns and definite noun phrase anaphors were interpreted more quickly if their antecedents were in the previous sentence, compared with the case where they were two or more sentences back. Two further experiments suggested that the crucial distinction was between the previous clause and clauses further back, rather than the previous sentence and more distant sentences. However, there was always a sentence boundary between the anaphor and its antecedent.

Garnham, Oakhill, and Cain (1998) examined the interpretation of verb phrase ellipses with antecedents in either the main or the subordinate clause of a preceding sentence, as in 6.55a–6.55d.

(6.55a) The art thieves might have taken both the Van Goghs from the gallery, if they hadn't set the alarm off, but fortunately they didn't.

(6.55b) If the art thieves hadn't set the alarm off, they might have taken both the Van Goghs from the gallery, but fortunately they didn't.

(6.55c) The art thieves might have taken both the Van Goghs from the gallery, if they hadn't set the alarm off, but fortunately they did.

(6.55d) If the art thieves hadn't set the alarm off, they might have taken both the Van Goghs from the gallery, but fortunately they did.

Previous work has shown that subordinate clauses are represented more superficially in immediate memory than main clauses (see in particular, Bever & Townsend, 1979; Townsend, 1983; Townsend & Bever, 1978, 1982). Garnham et al. found that ellipses were interpreted more quickly when they were one clause back than when they were two clauses back. They also found that they were easier to interpret when they were in elliptical clauses than in main clauses, so that an antecedent in a distant main clause was particularly difficult to interpret. Garnham et al. interpreted this result as reflecting the fact that a subordinate clause has to be held in short-term memory until its main clause has been processed, but a main clause may not have any subordinate clauses attached to it, and so does not have to be retained in a short-term store.

Knowledge-based factors

As was seen in an earlier example, repeated here in 6.56 and 6.57, the interpretation of a pronoun can be influenced by knowledge about the world.

(6.56) Sandra lied to Elaine during the trial because she was gullible.

(6.57) Sandra lied to Elaine during the trial because she was scared.

Indeed, many of the effects that will be described in detail later in this book (particularly in Chapters 8, 9, and 10) can be interpreted as effects of world knowledge on the interpretation of pronouns.

Marslen-Wilson, Tyler, and Koster (1993) investigated the effects of discourse focus, pragmatic inferences, and type of anaphor on discourse interpretation. They used a cross-modal naming task in which people had to say one of two visually presented pronouns (e.g., "him" or "her") after hearing a fragment such as "he overtook . . .". One pronoun was appropriate in the context, in this example "her", as the male protagonist in the preceding text was about to overtake a female. The subject of the fragment (the person referred to by "he" in this example) either was or was not the current discourse topic, and a pragmatic inference was needed to decide who did the overtaking if "he overtook . . ." was replaced by "overtaking . . .". Marslen-Wilson et al. showed that discourse focus alone could speed the naming of the pronoun consistent with assignment of the current focus to the agent of the fragment. More specifically, such speeded responding was found when there was no overt pronoun, and the verb did not provide any clue to which participant was performing the action ("waving at . . ."). They also showed that there was no difference between the case in which agency in the final fragment was assigned from an overt unambiguous pronoun ("he overtook . . .") and the case in which it was inferred from a zero anaphor and a biasing verb ("overtaking . . ."). Thus, unlike many previous studies, starting with Haviland and Clark (1974), Marslen-Wilson et al. found no evidence that pragmatic inferences make discourse integration more difficult.

Effects of world knowledge (or "plausibility") are also found in experiments in which people are asked to identify the referent of a pronoun (e.g., Caramazza, Grober, Garvey, & Yates, 1977; Hirst & Brill, 1980; Stevenson & Vitkovitch, 1986), even when there is a gender cue that determines what the pronoun refers to. Similar effects have been reported in studies in which clause reading times are measured (e.g., Garnham et al., 1992). However, in both of these tasks, the pronoun can be resolved before the end of the clause is read, so there is no guarantee that the effects of world knowledge are not occurring after pronoun assignment (see Sanford & Garrod, 1989, pp. 249–50, for a similar point).

SUMMARY

Once an anaphoric expression has been encountered in a text, the aspects of context relevant to its interpretation have to be identified, and an interpretation assigned to it. The interpretation derives in a (fairly) direct way from some aspect of the representation of the surrounding text and the context. The anaphor may either refer to the something already represented (identity of reference anaphora), or refer to another thing of the same kind (identity of sense anaphora). Psycholinguists have studied many factors that influence the interpretation of anaphoric expressions. These factors include morphology (gender, number, animacy, and case), syntax (and in particular the role of binding and command relations), the position of antecedent expressions in their clauses, the relation between the position of the antecedent expression and the anaphor (in particular the role of parallel function), the relation between the content of the anaphoric expression and the content of potential antecedent expressions, local and global focus, clause and sentence boundaries, and general knowledge. Strictly linguistic factors should win out over general knowledge, otherwise descriptions of unlikely situations are likely to be misinterpreted. General knowledge in turn should win out over heuristic strategies, such as parallel function and subject assignment, which people fall back on when there are no other cues to the interpretation of an anaphor.

CHAPTER SEVEN

Deep and surface anaphors

One of the most intriguing suggestions in the linguistic literature on anaphora is that there are two broad classes of anaphoric expression that share some properties (e.g., they obey the "backwards anaphora constraint" discussed in Chapter 4) but not others, and that these expressions are processed in different ways. The linguistic grounds for this distinction were discussed in detail by Hankamer and Sag (1976) and related to processing issues in a later paper (Sag & Hankamer, 1984). However, the distinction had been drawn earlier (e.g., Lakoff, 1975, originally circulated 1968).

THE LINGUISTIC DISTINCTION BETWEEN DEEP AND SURFACE ANAPHORS

Hankamer and Sag labelled the two classes of anaphoric expressions *deep* and *surface* anaphors. This terminology reflects the relation between the two types of anaphor and the deep and surface syntactic structures of sentences in Chomskyan transformational generative grammar. Hankamer and Sag's claim was that deep anaphors are interpreted by relating them to elements of deep structure, whereas surface anaphors are interpreted from surface structure. Sag and Hankamer (1984) suggested a more detailed processing theory for anaphoric expressions, one that related both to the traditional psycholinguistic distinction between representations of surface form and representations of content and, in the domain of content, to mental models theory.

All surface anaphors are elliptical structures. Indeed, Sag and Hankamer

(1984) renamed surface anaphors *ellipses*. However, not all (apparently) elliptical structures are surface anaphors, for example null complements (see Chapter 4) are not. Sag and Hankamer proposed that an ellipsis (of the surface anaphoric type) arises when a piece of text is missed out (elided) because its structure is identical to that of a nearby piece of text (its antecedent). In their 1984 paper they also argue that the level at which the structures have to be identical is not as superficial as Chomskyan surface structure. Perhaps the most compelling demonstration of this fact is that when one speaker's ellipsis has its antecedent in another speaker's contribution to a conversation, indexical expressions such as "you" and "me" swap around so that their referents remain the same (by the process of vehicle change mentioned in Chapter 4). So, if one speaker says 7.1a and the addressee replies with 7.1b the ellipsis means "give you my exam script".

(7.1a)   You must give me your exam script.
(7.1b)   No, I won't.

"Me" in the antecedent corresponds to "you" in the filled-out version of the ellipsis, and "your" to "my". However, "me" and "you" both refer to the first speaker and "your" and "my" to the second speaker.

From this observation and others Sag and Hankamer (1984) suggest that the superficial level of linguistic representation used to interpret ellipses is *logical form* (May, 1985), though the treatment of indexicals requires refinement of May's notion of logical form. This idea leads to the following principle, originally stated by Sag (1976):

Delete a VP [verb phrase] only if its logical translation is an alphabetic variant of some expression in the logical translation of the surrounding discourse.

The notion of an alphabetic variant is needed because in logical form it does not matter whether a bound variable is written as "x" or "y", as long as it is written the same way throughout a formula.

In comprehension, the problem in interpreting ellipses is to identify where material has been missed out, or elided, and to recover the meaning of the elliptical clause, as it would be if the material were in place. One plausible mechanism for recovering meaning is to find an appropriate piece of the representation of the logical form of the surrounding discourse, to copy it into the representation of the logical form of the elliptical clause, and to interpret the filled out elliptical clause as though it had been a full clause. On this view the meaning of the antecedent plays only an indirect role in the interpretation of the ellipsis. It is the *form* of the ellipsis that is copied, and the copy of the form is used to construct an interpretation for the elliptical clause.

In their 1984 paper Sag and Hankamer renamed deep anaphors as *model-interpretive* anaphors. The prototypical example of a model-interpretive anaphor is a definite pronoun, such as "he", "she", "it", or "they". According to Sag and Hankamer the interpretation of model-interpretive anaphors "involv[es] direct reference to constructs of the understander's discourse model" (1984, p. 335). On this view, the importance of the antecedent expression, if there is one, is that it introduced the relevant element into the discourse model: Anaphors are not interpreted by linking them directly to antecedent expressions. Cornish (1996) suggests that the linguistic expression should be called the *antecedent trigger*, to distinguish it from the antecedent proper, which is the referent of the definite pronoun. Cornish argues that the antecedent trigger need not be an expression that refers to the antecedent (see Chapter 4 for further discussion).

The different methods of interpreting ellipses and model-interpretive anaphors are linked to the two main criteria that Hankamer and Sag (1976) used to distinguish between deep and surface anaphors. The first is that surface anaphors require a *linguistic* antecedent, whereas deep anaphors do not. Deep anaphors can be under *pragmatic control*. For example, Hankamer and Sag contrast 7.2 and 7.3 (non-linguistic contexts shown in square brackets).

(7.2)   [Hankamer attempts to stuff a 9-inch ball through a 6-inch hoop]
        Sag: It's not clear that you'll be able to.

(7.3)   [Same context]
        Sag: It's not clear that you'll be able to do it.

They claim that Sag's utterance in 7.2 is "incompatible with the indicated context" (1976, p. 392, fn. 5), whereas his utterance in 7.3 is not. The difference is that in 7.2 Sag employs *verb phrase ellipsis* (VPE), which is a surface anaphor or ellipsis, whereas in 7.3 he uses "do it" anaphora, which is deep or model-interpretive, and thus may come under pragmatic, rather than linguistic, control. It can take its meaning directly from an element of non-linguistic context and does not, therefore, require a linguistic antecedent. If the copying account of the interpretation of surface anaphors is correct, the reason they need linguistic antecedents is that there has to be a linguistic form to copy.

The second criterion is that surface anaphors require their antecedents to have a linguistic form parallel to that of the ellided material. Deep anaphors, even when they have linguistic antecedents, do not require parallelism between the form of the antecedent and the form of the material that the anaphor can be regarded as replacing. Cornish's distinction between antecedent and antecedent trigger derives from cases where there is a relevant linguistic expression in the surrounding text, but where that expression cannot substitute for the anaphor and preserve the intended meaning. Hankamer and Sag contrast 7.4 and 7.5.

(7.4a)   Nobody else would take the oats down to the bin,
(7.4b)   so Bill did.
(7.4c)   so Bill did it.
(7.4d)   so Bill volunteered.

(7.5a)   The oats had to be taken down to the bin,
(7.5b)   so Bill did.
(7.5c)   so Bill did it.
(7.5d)   so Bill volunteered.

In each case, the version with (a) followed by (b) contains a verb phrase ellipsis, (a) followed by (c) has "do it", and (a) followed by (d) *null complement anaphora*, which is a model-interpretive. In each case the anaphor would mean "(to) take the oats down to the bin", which parallels the antecedent in 7.4, but not in 7.5. Hankamer and Sag claim that, in line with their predictions, 7.5a followed by 7.5b, the only case that has both a surface anaphor and a non-parallel antecedent, is not appropriate, but all the others are. If the copying account is correct, a parallel form must be copied, otherwise the filled out anaphor may have the wrong interpretation or no sensible interpretation at all ("Bill did be taken down to the bin"). As discussed in Chapter 4, later research has suggested that some cases of non-parallelism might be incorporated within a theory of the kind that Sag and Hankamer proposed.

The idea that the distinction between deep and surface anaphora is primarily a linguistic one has sometimes been challenged (e.g., Murphy, 1985b). Murphy argues that the distinction derives from a psychological property of anaphoric expressions, not a linguistic one: the ease of recoverability of their antecedents. However, he concedes that grammaticality judgements cannot always be explained by ease of recoverability, and suggests that the distinction has become grammaticalised. The resulting linguistic rules forbid cases of surface anaphora that would be hard to understand if there were no linguistic antecedent, but they also forbid cases such as 7.6, even though it has only one plausible interpretation, which interpretation is not difficult to derive.

(7.6)   The garbage needed to be taken out, so Sandy did.

PSYCHOLOGICAL RESEARCH ON DEEP
AND SURFACE ANAPHORS

Although Sag and Hankamer (1984) suggested a processing theory based on their distinction between ellipses and model-interpretive anaphors, the distinction itself is based on linguistic observations. Furthermore, those authors do not present experimental evidence to support their theory. The theory has many attractive features, and it links with the well-established distinction in psycholinguistics between short-lived representations of the superficial form of texts, and more permanent representations of their content.

Two sets of predictions follow from Sag and Hankamer's theory:

- From the requirement for parallel antecedents for ellipses, surface anaphors should be more difficult to interpret when they do not have a parallel antecedent than when they do. Presumably their interpretation in such cases would require the construction of an appropriate linguistic antecedent. This effect should not be observed for deep anaphors.
- Because representations of superficial form are short lived, surface anaphors should be more difficult to interpret when their antecedents are distant than when their antecedents are near. Because representations of content and context, from which deep anaphors are interpreted, are not so short lived, and do not necessarily have structures that correspond to that of the superficial form of the text, such *distance* effects are not expected for deep anaphors.

Both sets of predictions have been examined in detail. The results of these experimental studies have provided some support for Hankamer and Sag's distinction between deep and surface anaphor. However, the empirical findings have not supported their processing theory, elegant though it is.

Comparisons between deep and surface anaphors

Murphy (1985a) examined the effects of three variables on the interpretation of deep and surface verb phrase anaphors ("do it" and VPE): distance between antecedent and anaphor, length of antecedent, and parallelism of form between antecedent and anaphor. He found that increased length and non-parallelism slowed the interpretation of *both* types of anaphors, although the effects of these two factors were restricted to cases in which the antecedent was in the immediately preceding sentence. More particularly, there was no evidence that deep and surface anaphors are interpreted differently, contrary to the claims of Hankamer and Sag. The results do, however, suggest that there are different processes for interpreting anaphoric expressions. When their antecedents are close, surface features of the text affect their interpretation, suggesting a copying process of the kind described previously, or some other process that makes use of a representation of superficial form. However, when the antecedents of anaphoric expressions are more distant, a process based on content and plausible reasoning appears to come into play.

Tanenhaus and his colleagues have reported a different set of findings, and they have also suggested some complications in the interpretation of Murphy's results. First, an effect of the length of the antecedent does not provide unequivocal evidence for the use of superficial form. As Tanenhaus and Carlson (1990) point out, longer antecedents can introduce ambiguities of interpretation. Furthermore, a longer antecedent will have a more complex conceptual representation, which may be more difficult to access and use in the process of anaphor interpretation. The lack of a length effect when material intervenes between the antecedent and the anaphor is more difficult to interpret from this perspective. However, Tanenhaus and Carlson argue that Murphy's distance effect is also problematic, because of a confounding factor in the distant condition.

As is known from studies of NP-anaphora (e.g., Lesgold et al., 1979), material intervening between an anaphor and its antecedent can produce "distance" effects that are attributable to a change in focus. When the intervening material does not change the focus, such distance effects are reduced or eliminated. Tanenhaus, Carlson, and Seidenberg (1985) report a distance effect for a surface anaphor (sluicing) but no effect for a corresponding deep anaphor ("do it"). In this experiment the intervening sentences were statives, which did not change the focus as, for example, in 7.7.

(7.7a)   Someone has to paint the garage.
(7.7b)   The paint is peeling and the wood is beginning to rot.
(7.7c)   Let's take a vote and see who.
(7.7d)   Let's take a vote and see who has to do it.

Tanenhaus and Carlson suggest that the intervening material in Murphy's passages may have shifted the focus away from the VP anaphor's antecedent, so that the relative difficulty of interpreting the deep anaphor in the distance condition was caused by having to reinstate the antecedent, and not because of distance *per se* (Murphy, 1985a does not provide examples of the intervening material).

Tanenhaus and Carlson (1990) also report, unlike Murphy, an interaction between anaphor type and parallelism of antecedent and anaphor. However, this interaction was found in the number of positive judgements about whether the anaphor-containing sentence made sense as a continuation of the passage, a measure that Murphy did not take. When Tanenhaus and Carlson looked at times to make positive judgements, they found a main effect of parallelism, but no interaction with type of anaphor, just as Murphy had.

A later study (Mauner, Tanenhaus, & Carlson, 1995a) examined in more detail one way in which Tanenhaus and Carlson had manipulated parallelism: the use of a passivised antecedent (Tanenhaus & Carlson, 1990, Exp. 1). Mauner et al. found that the parallelism effects on the time taken to accept deep anaphors were restricted to full passives (with agentive "by" phrases) and were not found with truncated passives. A further experiment, in which the type of passive was systematically varied, confirmed this finding. Unfortunately, Mauner et al. do not suggest a definitive account of this result, nor of why a different way of manipulating parallelism (nominalisation of a verb phrase, Tanenhaus & Carlson, 1990, Exp. 2) also produced an effect on times taken to make positive judgements for deep anaphors.

Murphy (1990) also tried to resolve the conflict between his previous results and those of Tanenhaus and his colleagues. He suggested that the interaction between type of anaphor and distance reported by Tanenhaus et al. (1985) might be explained by the fact that the surface anaphor had a potential (if implausible) antecedent in the intervening sentence, but the deep anaphor did not. In the passage about painting the garage, 7.7c could, according to morphosyntactic constraints, mean 7.8.

(7.8)   Let's take a vote and see who is peeling.

However, it is not possible to take the "do it" version, 7.7d to mean 7.9, because "do it" cannot have a stative antecedent.

(7.9)   Let's take a vote and see who has to be peeling.

Murphy carried out a study in which he systematically varied the ambiguity of the ellipsis, using different versions of the intervening material, However, he found no evidence for an effect of ambiguity.

Murphy also compared the results of this study, in which people answered yes/no questions following the passages, with the results of a similar study in which they made judgements about whether the sentence containing the anaphor was a sensible continuation of the passage. He found that judgement times were affected by distance for the surface anaphors, but not for the deep anaphors. The reading times, however, had shown distance effects for both deep and surface anaphors. The pattern of results reported by Tanenhaus et al. (1985) was similar to that reported by Murphy for his judgement task, but they do not provide details of the task in their experiment. Murphy argues that the "makes sense" task, which requires people to make metalinguistic judgements, is more likely to produce data that parallels the judgements of linguists. However, because linguistically unacceptable anaphors (e.g., surface anaphors with non-parallel antecedents) are often easy to interpret, simple comprehension tasks may show effects that do not reflect linguistic judgements.

Jakimik and Glenberg (1990) studied the interpretation of temporal anaphors, such as "the latter approach", and ordinary noun phrase anaphors, such as "the medical approach", which they called semantically based anaphors. They found that temporal anaphors were more easily resolved in spoken than in written discourse, whereas semantically based anaphors were not. This result is consistent with Glenberg and Swanson's (1986) temporal distinctiveness theory, and is related by Jakimik and Glenberg to Hankamer and Sag's (1976) distinction between surface and deep anaphors, since the interpretation of an expression like "the latter" depends on surface characteristics of the text.

The interpretation surface anaphors

As the studies described earlier showed, surface anaphors, if not deep anaphors, show distance effects even when there is no change of focus. However, passages such as the one from Tanenhaus et al. (1985), repeated here in 7.10, do not sound entirely natural, even if focus is maintained.

(7.10a)   Someone has to paint the garage.
(7.10b)   The paint is peeling and the wood is beginning to rot.
(7.10c)   Let's take a vote and see who (has to do it).

Garnham (1987) used similar passages to Tanenhaus et al., with stative intervening clauses, for example 7.11, and found similar distance effects for the surface anaphor VP-ellipsis.

(7.11a)   Margie wanted the recipes.
(7.11b)   The main dish was mouthwatering.
(7.11c)   The dessert was delicious.
(7.11d)   Tom did, too.

In a second experiment the passages were altered to make them sound more natural, while maintaining the distance between the anaphor and its antecedent, for example 7.12.

(7.12a)   Margie wanted the recipes,
(7.12b)   because the main dish was mouthwatering,
(7.12c)   and the dessert was delicious.
(7.12d)   Tom did, too.

Judgement data showed that adding the conjunctions increased the rated naturalness of the passages in the distant condition (from 61% to 88% of ellipses rated as acceptable continuations of the passages). However, the times to make positive judgements showed a distance effect that did not interact with the presence or absence of conjunctions.

Although Garnham's experiment failed to show an effect of discourse structure on the time taken to make positive judgements about ellipses, a study by Malt (1985) did show that (other) aspects of discourse structure can have such effects. For example, an elliptical verb phrase that is part of an answer to a previously asked question, as in 7.13, is interpreted more easily than one that conveys the same information, but not as part of a question and answer sequence, as in 7.14 (Malt, 1985, Exp. 1).

(7.13a) Everyone was returning from vacation.
(7.13b) "Did Greg see Maureen and Marjorie last night?" Helen asked.
(7.13c) "I think they just got back in town."
(7.13d) "Yes, he did," Sophia replied.

(7.14a) Everyone was returning from vacation.
(7.14b) "Greg saw Maureen and Marjorie last night" Helen remarked.
(7.14c) "I think they just got back in town."
(7.14d) "Yes, he did," Sophia replied.

Similarly, an interpolation by another speaker, as in 7.15, makes a question less available as a source of the antecedent for an ellipsis than if the speaker who asks the question makes the same remark as an additional comment on the question, as in 7.16 (Malt, 1985, Exp. 4).

(7.15a) Andrea was anxious to leave the house.
(7.15b) "Aren't we going to the game?" she asked.
(7.15c) "It's getting kind of late," Brian observed.
(7.15d) "Yes, we are," Ray assured her.

(7.16a) Andrea was anxious to leave the house.
(7.16b) "Aren't we going to the game?" she asked.
(7.16c) "It's getting kind of late," she added.
(7.16d) "Yes, we are," Ray assured her.

Garnham and Oakhill (1987) investigated the idea, implicit in Sag and Hankamer's theory of the interpretation of ellipses, that the meaning of the surrounding text is not directly implicated in this process. Sag and Hankamer proposed that ellipses are interpreted by copying a piece of logical form representing part of the text surrounding (usually preceding) the ellipsis, and then interpreting that piece of logical form in its new context. If this account is correct, the only effects of content should be those that arise during that final interpretation process. Garnham and Oakhill constructed passages in which a possible (and plausible) meaning for an ellipsis was in some sense available from context, but not as part of the representation of the logical form of the piece of text that should be copied into the ellipsis. For example, they used passages such as 7.17.

(7.17a) It had been a busy morning in the hospital.
(7.17b) The elderly patient had been examined by the doctor during the ward round.
(7.17c) The child/nurse had too.

In the version with "child", the ellipsis is correctly interpreted to mean "had been examined by the doctor". However, in the version with "nurse", it is more plausible that the nurse had examined the elderly patient during the ward round than that the nurse had been examined by the doctor during the ward round. In these circumstances, the interpretation of the ellipsis was frequently incorrect, as shown by answers to questions such as 7.18.

(7.18) Did the doctor examine the nurse?

Even when the answers were correct, they were produced slowly. These results show that the interpretation of an ellipsis is affected by a content-based representation, and is not achieved by copying a piece of logical form, and then interpreting it in the position of the ellipsis. In other words, representations of both linguistic form and content (mental models) contribute to the interpretation of ellipses, contrary to Sag and Hankamer.

However, when passages are not deliberately made misleading, representations of surface form play an important role in the interpretation of ellipses. Frazier and Clifton (1998) examined the interpretation of sluiced clauses and provided evidence for the use of logical form rather than a mental model in their interpretation. They investigated cases of sluicing with what they called explicit and implicit antecedents, for example 7.19 and 7.20.

(7.19) The secretary typed something but I don't know what.

(7.20) The secretary typed but I don't know what.

They found that the sluiced clause was read more quickly when the antecedent was explicit. This finding held both when the antecedent was an argument of the verb in the first clause, as in 7.19 and 7.20, and when it was an adjunct, as in 7.21 and 7.22.

(7.21) The secretary typed somewhere but I don't know where.

(7.22)   The secretary typed but I don't know where.

Mauner, Tanenhaus, and Carlson (1995b) had previously shown that implicit arguments (but presumably not implicit adjuncts) can aid the understanding of following clauses. Frazier and Clifton, therefore, explain their findings by assuming that sluicing is interpreted at the level of logical form, as proposed by Chung, Ladusaw, and McCloskey (1995), but that implicit arguments are only represented in a discourse representation (or mental model).

The interpretation deep anaphors

If representations of content are used to interpret ellipses, as Garnham and Oakhill (1987) showed, representations of surface form may be used to interpret model-interpretive anaphors. As discussed earlier, Murphy (1985a) argued that superficial representations play a role in the understanding of deep verb phrase anaphors, though the confound with focus compromises the interpretation of this result. Pronouns and definite noun phrase anaphors are more typical deep anaphors, and several studies have attempted to show that surface form plays a role in their interpretation.

Cloitre and Bever (1988) concluded that "pronouns provide direct access to a conceptual representation of the antecedent, whereas repeated noun anaphors do so indirectly, priming a surface (lexical) level of representation as a preliminary to accessing the conceptual representation" (1988, p. 293, abstract). In other words, they claim that Sag and Hankamer were correct for pronominal anaphors, but not for noun phrase anaphors. Cloitre and Bever used passages such as 7.23.

(7.23a)   The gangly busboy spilled soup on the famous actress.
(7.23b)   A waiter ran to help the busboy/him.

Following these passages, people were asked to respond to the word "gangly". In different experiments the responses were probe word recognition, lexical decision, and category decision (abstract versus concrete). Noun phrase anaphors produced more facilitation in lexical decision, whereas pronominal anaphors produced more facilitation in category decision. Cloitre and Bever argued that responses in lexical decision rely more on surface than conceptual features, whereas the reverse is true for responses in category decision.

Lucas, Tanenhaus, and Carlson (1990) came to a different conclusion from Cloitre and Bever. They compared lexical decision and naming responses to probes following passages such as 7.24.

(7.24a)   Sarah could not decide whether to buy steak or hamburger.

(7.24b)   She finally chose the more/less expensive meat.
(7.24c)   The store has a wide selection of foods.
(7.24d)   PROBE: steak

According to Lucas et al., lexical decision is sensitive to both superficial and conceptual representations, whereas naming is sensitive only to superficial representations. They interpret their results, which show facilitation in the appropriate case (. . . "more expensive meat . . . steak . . .") only for lexical decision and not for naming, as showing that noun phrase anaphors are interpreted from elements in discourse models.

Garnham et al. (1995) suggest a way to reconcile these results. They propose that, when an anaphor is close to its antecedent, as in the passages used by Cloitre and Bever and by Lucas et al., superficial form will be used to interpret the anaphor if possible, even if the anaphor is a model-interpretive one. Both sets of authors agree that pronouns are interpreted from a conceptual representation, not a superficial one. However, in English most definite pronouns cannot be interpreted by using their superficial features to link to an antecedent expression. In this respect the passage cited earlier from Cloitre and Bever, in which the masculine form "he" matches the masculine "boy" in "busboy" is atypical not only of English definite pronouns, but of Cloitre and Bever's own set of materials. Most English pronouns do not match their antecedents at a superficial level. They are therefore unlikely to reactivate directly the superficial features of their antecedent expressions.

This argument also explains why Lucas et al. failed to find an effect of superficial representations in the interpretation of noun phrase anaphors. Their noun phrase anaphors (e.g., "the more expensive meat") did not match their antecedent expressions (e.g., "steak") at a superficial level, and therefore could not reactivate the antecedent expression by superficial matching. Thus, across both sets of studies, in the only condition in which a superficial representation could plausibly have aided anaphor interpretation (Cloitre and Bever's NP anaphor condition in which the noun, e.g., "busboy", was repeated), it did.

Garnham et al. (1995), following work by Carreiras, Garnham, and Oakhill (1993), provided evidence for the use of superficial representations in the interpretation of definite pronouns in a different way. It is well established that, in English, a pronoun that can be interpreted from its gender is easier to process than one that requires other, usually inferential, processes to interpret it. For example, Garnham and Oakhill (1985) presented sentences such as 7.25 and 7.26.

(7.25)   Alan lent a pen to Jill because she wanted to write a letter.

(7.26)   Vicky lent a pen to Jill because she wanted to write a letter.

They showed that the second clause of 7.25, in which the pronoun "she" refers to Jill, because Jill is the only female character introduced into the brief narrative, is read more quickly than the second clause of 7.26, in which the referent of "she" has to be determined from who ends up with an object that is lent and whether a person needs to acquire or give away a pen to write a letter.

This *gender cueing* effect, which has been reported in many other studies (e.g., Caramazza et al., 1977; McDonald & MacWhinney, 1995, Vonk, 1985a, b), cannot be unambiguously interpreted in English, because the morphological gender of English definite pronouns is (almost entirely) confounded with the gender of their referents. Matching could take place using either morphological or semantic information about the pronoun. Indeed, because most English nouns are not morphologically marked for gender it is most likely that matching occurs at a semantic level. Carreiras et al. (1993) point out that in many other languages nouns and noun phrases are often morphologically marked for gender, and that for inanimate noun phrases those morphological markings are not confounded with semantic information, because inanimate objects do not have semantic gender. Thus matching between a French feminine noun phrase such as "la table" (the table) and a following co-referential pronoun "elle" (it, feminine) can only be morphosyntactic matching.

Carreiras et al. (1993) showed that such morphological matching effects speed the interpretation of Spanish definite pronouns. However the interpretation of their results was complicated because Spanish is a pro-drop language in which subject pronouns do not usually appear, and their only experiment with object pronouns (1993, Exp. 3) did not contain a direct comparison between pronouns referring to objects and pronouns referring to people. Garnham et al. (1995) did make such a comparison and also conducted an experiment in French, which is not a pro-drop language. They showed that matching effects were no smaller for references to objects (where the matching can only be performed on a morphosyntactic basis) than for references to people (where it can be performed on either a morphosyntactic or a semantic basis). Thus, although the distinction between deep and surface anaphors may be defensible on linguistic grounds, it appears that Sag and Hankamer's processing theory, attractive though it is, is incorrect.

SUMMARY

Linguists have distinguished between two types of anaphor: surface anaphors or ellipses and deep or model-interpretive anaphors. The distinction was studied in detail by Hankamer and Sag (1976), who based a processing theory on the distinction (Sag & Hankamer, 1984). Sag and Hankamer suggested that ellipses take their interpretation from a superficial level of representation of discourse (possibly the logical form of individual clauses) and model-interpretive anaphors take their interpretation from a deeper representation (possibly a discourse model). Although the linguistic theory provides a good account of considered grammaticality (or appropriateness) judgements, the processing theory based on the linguistic distinction is almost certainly incorrect. Psychologists have directly compared the two types of anaphor, but evidence that they are processed differently has been equivocal. The clearest evidence for differences in the behaviour of the two types of anaphor is found in tasks where people make explicit judgements similar to the ones made by linguists. Furthermore, it has been shown that representations of surface form and representations of content are used in the understanding of both types of anaphoric expression.

CHAPTER EIGHT

Anaphoric islands

This chapter discusses a class of cases in which an anaphor, usually a definite pronoun, has a meaning that does not correspond in a straightforward way to the meaning of another expression in the surrounding text. The cases in question are references into so-called *anaphoric islands*. When a definite pronoun refers into an anaphoric island there is no co-referential antecedent expression. Consider, for example, 8.1.

(8.1)   They had a feature on violent youngsters, attributing it to drink.

In this sentence "it" refers to violence in youngsters, yet the previous related expression (the antecedent trigger in Cornish's, 1996 terminology) refers to the youngsters themselves, and violent is a property that is predicated of them. From the perspective of text comprehension, the question arises of how the meaning of the anaphoric expression is computed. More specifically, from the mental models viewpoint, the question is how and when does violence, the referent of "it", become represented in the mental model. In particular, is it represented when the property of being violent is mentioned, or only when the pronoun "it" has to be interpreted as referring to violence?

WHAT IS AN "ANAPHORIC ISLAND"?

The term "anaphoric island" requires explanation. The notion of an island was introduced into generative linguistics in the 1960s, largely as a result of research reported in Ross's (1967) dissertation, *Constraints on Variables in*

Syntax, later published as Ross (1986). In the generative grammar of the 1960s, which derived from the so-called *standard theory* of Chomsky's (1965) *Aspects of the Theory of Syntax*, sentences were thought of as generated (in an abstract, not a psychological, sense) from underlying or *deep* structures in which relations between their parts were represented in a uniform and explicit manner. *Surface* structures of sentences were derived by operations that moved, deleted, or otherwise changed elements in the underlying structure. Ross argued that there are certain structures out of which elements cannot be moved. Rules that specify movement cannot refer to parts of these structures if they also refer to material outside them. They can only operate either wholly outside the structures, or wholly within them. Ross refers to such structures as *islands*, and the constraints on movement rules as *island constraints*.

Within generative grammar, an account of where anaphoric expressions can occur in sentences was conceived as a set of rules (transformational or otherwise) relating anaphoric expressions to antecedent expressions that licensed their occurrence. Postal (1969) argued that there are cases in which such rules cannot relate two linguistic expressions one of which is within a particular structure and one of which is outside it. He, therefore, adapted Ross's terminology and called such structures anaphoric islands, and the prohibition on anaphoric relations across the boundaries of such structures the *anaphoric island constraint.*

The structures that Postal had in mind were words. For example, an orphan is, by definition, a child that has lost its parents. It may, therefore, seem surprising that processing the word "orphan" does not make readily available—and hence available for pronominal reference—(a representation of) the parents of the person described as an orphan. Indeed, in the particular version of generative grammar favoured by Postal, generative semantics, it *was* surprising. In generative semantics word meanings are assembled from components of meaning in the derivation of a sentence, and lexical items are substituted for collections of meaning components in the derivation of the surface structure of a sentence. So, within that framework, Postal (1969) was forced to propose the anaphoric island constraint. Otherwise, before "parents" is put together with "dead" and other components of meaning, it should be possible to make the pronoun "them" co-refer with "parents". The constraint effectively filters out, at a late stage in their generation, sentences such as 8.2, in which "them" is intended to refer to Max's parents.

(8.2)   Max is an orphan and he deeply misses them.

In fact, Postal was able to turn the existence of anaphoric islands into an argument for generative semantics. He argued that words were anaphoric islands, and resisted both anaphoric references that are *outbound* from part of the word to an anaphoric expression, and also anaphoric references that are *inbound*, where the anaphoric element is part of the word. For example, it is not possible to say 8.3.

(8.3)   People who smoke like other do soers.

Postal claimed that the anaphoric island constraint, acting as a late filter on well-formedness, provided a uniform account of the unacceptability of both outbound and inbound anaphora, whereas alternative theories had to postulate separate accounts for the two cases.

Although generative semantics never inspired psycholinguistic theories, either of comprehension or production, it would be natural to think of comprehension from a generative semantics point of view as, among other things, a process in which word meanings are decomposed into their component parts. Such decompositional theories have also been suggested within an interpretive semantic theory, for example in the account of word meaning developed by Katz and Fodor (1963) and in feature-based psychological theories (e.g., Schaeffer & Wallace, 1969; Smith, Shoben, & Rips, 1974) that derive in part from Katz and Fodor's views.

Despite the apparent attractiveness of these views, psychological attempts to find evidence for semantic decomposition of word meanings as an automatic component of comprehension were unsuccessful (Johnson-Laird, 1983, pp. 207–211; Kintsch, 1974). There was no evidence that the semantic complexity of a word affected how difficult it was to process. However, a different line of work showed that components of a word's meaning could be processed separately. For example, Johnson-Laird, Gibbs, and de Mowbray (1978) asked people to decide whether words named members of a class with three defining characteristics (natural, consumable, solid, for example "apple"). In a later unexpected memory test, memory for words in the original list increased as a function of the number of components of meaning shared with the target category.

Similarly, Tabossi and Johnson-Laird (1980) presented people with different sentences containing the same word, and showed that different sentences made different aspects of a word's meaning available. For example, 8.4a relates to the hardness of diamonds, whereas 8.4b relates to their brilliance, and no particular characteristic of diamonds is relevant to the interpretation of 8.4c.

(8.4a)   The goldsmith cut the glass with the diamond.
(8.4b)   The mirror dispersed the light from the diamond.
(8.4c)   The film showed the person with the diamond.
(8.4d)   Is a diamond hard?
(8.4e)   Is a diamond brilliant?

Question 8.4d was answered more quickly after 8.4a, and 8.4e more quickly after 8.4b. Times for both questions following 8.4c were intermediate. This effect of sentence context on the aspects of a word's meaning that become available is related to the phenomenon of instantiation of nouns (Anderson et al., 1976) and verbs (Garnham, 1979). For example, people take the container in 8.5 to be a basket and the detecting in 8.6 to be smelling.

(8.5)   The container held the apples

(8.6)   The servant detected the gas.

Within the framework sketched in Chapter 4 these findings are not surprising. The degree to which mental models are elaborated depends on both the purposes of the reader and the links that have to be made with other pieces of information. If something is described as "a diamond" and someone uses it for cutting, its hardness becomes relevant. However, if someone is described as an orphan, the model may simply record that the predicate "is an orphan" applies to that person. Nevertheless, this specific piece of information in the mental model will have a link to an address in semantic memory associated with that predicate and, hence, it will have indirect links to those parts of semantic memory that encode the meaning of the predicate and that encode both general and specific knowledge about orphans. Thus, it is possible for information about an orphan having dead parents to be made available. Indeed, because there is a strong (definitional) link between being an orphan and having dead parents, it is plausible that such information will be available.

What the mental models theory does suggest is that, unless or until it is important for the reader or listener to focus on the parents of someone who is described as an orphan, those parents may not be represented, or at least not strongly represented in the model of the text. Since they are not strongly represented, a pronominal reference to them is generally inappropriate. However, since an orphan is defined by the death of his or her parents, an anaphoric reference to them using a full noun phrase is appropriate. It might indeed be no more difficult to understand than if they had been explicitly mentioned, as in Garrod and Sanford's (1981) study where clothes were referred to without difficulty following a mention of someone dressing a baby (see Chapters 3 and 6). In this case, as with the parents of the orphan, the appropriate anaphor for referring to the clothes was a definite noun phrase, not a pronoun.

Postal's (1969) original claim was that references into anaphoric islands are always unacceptable, even when the intended interpretation of the anaphor and the antecedent (trigger) are morphologically related, which they are not in the "orphan/parents" case. For example, Postal considered both 8.7 and 8.8 to be ungrammatical.

(8.7)   McCarthyites are now puzzled by his intentions.

(8.8)   Smokers really shouldn't do so.

However, later authors (e.g., Corum, 1973; Lakoff & Ross, 1972) argued that references into anaphoric islands are more acceptable when the natural way of referring to the intended antecedent uses an expression that is morphologically related to the island itself. Lakoff and Ross also claimed that the syntactic relation between the antecedent (trigger) and the anaphor determined how acceptable the anaphoric reference was. For example, they claimed that 8.9 is less acceptable than 8.10, because the antecedent trigger ("guitarist") in 8.9 *commands* (see Chapter 4) the pronoun "it", whereas in 8.10 it does not.

(8.9)   The guitarist thought that it was a beautiful instrument.

(8.10)   John became a guitarist because he thought it was a beautiful instrument.

Corum considered examples such as 8.11.

(8.11)   Shakespearean imitators usually fail to capture his style.

In such cases, even if the use of the adjectival "Shakespearean" does not introduce a representation of Shakespeare the person directly into the model, the connection to Shakespeare is close. Corum argued that (at least in some dialects of English) a pronoun can refer to part of the semantic structure of a word, and she used this fact to construct another argument in favour of generative semantics.

Tic Douloureux (1971) argued for a special class of exceptions to the anaphoric island constraint, and in particular that:

> Whenever a sentence has a semantic interpretation making reference to an action or event that [inferentially] results in the production of an unmentionable bodily substance, such a substance can be referred to by a pronoun "it" within the sentence, and indeed an otherwise antecedentless "it" in such a disgusting environment usually takes such an interpretation. (1971, p. 48)

Tic Douloureux argues that this constraint explains the acceptability of sentences such as 8.12.

(8.12)   John bled so much it soaked through his bandage and stained his shirt.

Interestingly, although the action or event is defined by the substance, so that the substance is part of the meaning of the verb, the most natural way of referring to the substance is not necessarily morphologically related to the verb. For example, in 8.13 the substance is most obviously sick or vomit, though it might be referred to as "what little Johnny threw up".

(8.13)   When little Johnny threw up, was there any pencil-eraser in it?

A more serious set of observations was made by Browne (1974), who showed that reference into an anaphoric island required only a semantic (and morphological) relation between the anaphoric "island" and the natural interpretation of the pronoun, not, as Postal (1969), Corum (1973) and others had claimed, a part–whole relation between the meaning of the anaphor and the meaning of the antecedent trigger. Thus, it is possible to say both 8.14 and 8.15.

(8.14)   Even those who were not dogmatic surrealists were influenced by its spirit.

(8.15)   Surrealism was new and appealing partly because they were acquainted with Freud's discoveries about dreams.

If "surrealism" is part of the meaning of "surrealist" (an adherent of surrealism), the reverse relation cannot also hold.

Browne's observations have implications for processing theories (as well as linguistic theories), over and above those of the earlier accounts that claimed that the meaning of the anaphoric expression should be part of the meaning of the antecedent expression (and that the two should be morphologically related). For comprehension, if the meaning of the antecedent contains the meaning of the anaphoric expression as a proper part, interpreting the anaphoric expression could be a process that relies in a straightforward way on the representation of the surrounding, usually preceding, text. This idea would be particularly appealing in the context of generative semantics. If a word's meaning were already decomposed into its parts, using a part of the meaning to interpret an anaphoric expression should be no more difficult than using any other part of the sentence (e.g., syntactic relations) to interpret another part.

However, if Browne is correct, all that is required semantically for a successful reference into an anaphoric island is that some semantic relation, which might for example be either part–whole or whole–part, holds between the anaphor and its antecedent (or antecedent trigger) within the anaphoric island. On this view the process of interpretation is likely to make only indirect use, if any use at all, of linguistic structure. Even if a word's meaning is decomposed in the representation of a sentence in which it occurs, and it was noted earlier that such decomposition does not occur routinely, other related meanings, even those of morphologically related words, will not be represented. If it is possible to refer pronominally to surrealism, following a mention of surrealists, and also to refer pronominally to surrealists following a mention of surrealism, a more plausible account of what happens in processing is that the referent of the pronoun is *inferred* when the pronoun is encountered. However, if this idea is correct, the question arises of why a morphological relation between the anaphoric expression and the antecedent trigger is important. Indeed the question arises of what effect this relation has.

A later approach attempted to explain anaphoric island data within the theories of lexical morphology and phonology (e.g., Monahan, 1986). According to these theories syntactic processes do not have access to the internal structure of words. Thus, if anaphoric relations are syntactic relations, and many linguists believe they are, at least when antecedent and anaphor are in the same sentence, the prohibition on reference into anaphoric islands follows from the so-called *lexical integrity* hypothesis of lexical morphology, and need not be stated separately. However, like Postal's original anaphoric island constraint, this idea both claims that anaphoric islands are an all-or-none phenomenon, and rules out cases, primarily those in which the anaphor and its antecedent (trigger) are related morphologically, that many people find perfectly acceptable.

Ward, Sproat, and McKoon (1991) argue that although inbound reference into anaphoric islands is ruled out by syntactic principles, outbound reference, the type that is the subject of this chapter, is governed entirely by pragmatic constraints (except for "do so", which they claim is subject to a grammatical constraint on the nature of its antecedent). Ward et al. also suggest that a morphological relation between antecedent and anaphor is not necessary for reference into an anaphoric island. In one type of case reference is parasitic on morphological relations in related sentences. For example, in 8.16 "as many" means fourteen, which is clearly related to "fourteenth".

(8.16)   This is the fourteenth time in as many weeks.

However, although "second" and "two" are not morphologically related, 8.17 works just as well as 8.16.

(8.17)   This is the second time in as many weeks

Ward et al. also suggest that, if the pragmatic constraints are strong enough, references of the "... orphan ... them ..." type may be possible, even though there is no morphological relation and no corresponding paradigm. They cite an example from a novel in which such a reference follows the discussion of mothers, but with no explicit mention of "parents".

PSYCHOLOGICAL WORK ON ANAPHORIC ISLANDS

There has been little empirical work on the interpretation of references into anaphoric islands. In a pioneering study, Garnham and Oakhill (1988) presented brief texts, such as 8.18a or 8.18b followed by 8.18c.

(8.18a)   Young Toby gets into fights every playtime,
(8.18b)   Young Toby fights every playtime,
(8.18c)   but they never lead to injuries.

8.18a contains an ordinary NP antecedent "fights" for the pronoun "they" in 8.18c, but when 8.18c follows 8.18b "they" has to be interpreted as referring into an anaphoric island. People judged whether 8.18c was an appropriate continuation from 8.18a and 8.18b, and their judgements were timed. There were fewer positive judgements with 8.18b than with 8.18a (54% versus 92%), and those positive judgements were made more slowly. In a second experiment (Garnham & Oakhill, 1988, Exp. 2) the passages were shifted into the past tense, so that "fights" the plural noun was no longer identical to the verb form, which became "fought" rather than "fights", as in 8.19.

(8.19a)   Young Toby got into fights every playtime,
(8.19b)   Young Toby fought every playtime,
(8.19c)   but they never led to injuries.

This manipulation further reduced the number of positive judgements for references into anaphoric islands (to 29%). However, the difference in the times to make positive judgements between the noun phrase antecedent cases and the cases of reference into anaphoric islands remained the same (about 400 ms).

One interesting aspect of this result is that it provides further evidence for the use of representations of superficial form in the interpretation of deep anaphors (see Chapter 7). The number of positive judgements was affected by whether there was a superficial match between the form of the verb that is the anaphoric island (e.g., "fights" or "fought") and that of the noun (e.g., "fights").

Garnham and Oakhill (1988) concluded from this study that, even when a text mentions the activity of fighting, using the verb "to fight", a set of fights is not introduced in the mental model, and therefore the pronoun "they" cannot refer to these fights without their existence being inferred. They suggested that the extra 400 ms to make positive judgements about the references into anaphoric island was needed to make the relevant inferences.

More recent studies by Oakhill, Garnham, Cain, and Reynolds (2000a) and Garnham, Oakhill, and Reynolds (2000) have cast doubt on this conclusion. If the pronominal anaphor, "they" is replaced by the noun phrase anaphor "the fights", references into anaphoric islands do not take longer to understand than anaphoric references with standard noun phrase antecedents. This finding parallels that of Garrod and Sanford (1981) and suggests that an inference (to the existence of fights) is not necessary following a reference to the activity of fighting, perhaps because the activity of fighting has fights as part of its definition. If this conclusion is correct, the slowing down in the pronominal anaphor case must be attributed to the somewhat unsatisfactory nature of the passages even when, in a forced choice judgement, people judge a passage to be acceptable.

Other experiments by Oakhill et al.(2000a) and Garnham et al. (2000) examined the effect of distance between an anaphor and its antecedent on the interpretation of references into anaphoric islands. In these experiments people were asked to read passages such as 8.20, in which the antecedent is three clauses back from the anaphor, and 8.21, in which the antecedent is in the immediately preceding clause.

(8.20)   At night the cat scratches/makes scratches on the paintwork
and all the best furniture in the sitting-room,
which is a horrible nuisance.
They are difficult to polish off.

(8.21)   I took in a stray cat last week,
something which I am now regretting.
At night the cat scratches/makes scratches on the paintwork.
They are difficult to polish off.

The passages were matched for length, because mixing passages of different lengths produced an initially uninterpretable inverse effect of distance (judgements after long passages with distant antecedents were faster than judgements after short passages with close antecedents). This effect was attributable to the fact that, in the short passages, people could not be sure they were reading the line of the passage about which they had to judge whether it was a plausible continuation, but when they reached the fourth line of a passage they knew it had to be the last.

The results of these studies were that distance made passages with noun phrase antecedents less acceptable, and times for positive judgements increased. However, passages with distant verb phrase antecedents were more acceptable, and positive judgements were made more quickly, than with close verb phrase antecedents, particularly when the intervening material was written to avoid changes in focus (see Chapters 6 and 7). These results suggest that when a verbal antecedent is close, there is evidence from the surface representation that the passage is not correctly written, but as the antecedent becomes more distant it is more difficult to remember exactly how the text was worded, and hence less likely that information about the wording will interfere with the construction of the plausible message that these passages convey. To the extent that backgrounding effects were not entirely eliminated, as suggested by the residual distance effects for noun phrase antecedents, the improved ratings and speed of interpretation for verbal antecedents are partly masked by distance effects.

McKoon, Ward, Ratcliff, and Sproat (1993) compared anaphoric reference to, for example, deer using the pronoun "they", when the antecedent was either "hunting deer" or "deer hunting". In the first case "deer" is the head of an NP that provides a standard antecedent for "they", whereas in the second case "deer" is a modifier of "hunting" and the reference is into an anaphoric island. Using a probe word detection task (probing for "deer"), McKoon et al. found no difference in response time following passages containing "deer hunting" and passages containing "hunting deer". The self-paced reading times for the pronoun-containing sentences were faster following "hunting deer" than following "deer hunting". However, this effect was eliminated when the preceding passage was closely related to the topic of deer hunting (when it was about someone who liked fishing and shooting, rather than about someone who liked outdoor activities, such as ski-ing and mountain climbing, in general). The overall pattern of results suggests that "deer" is available after either version of the passage is read, but that a pronominal reference to deer following "deer hunting" is only fully acceptable if context provides strong support.

SUMMARY

The notion of an anaphoric island was introduced into the linguistic literature by Postal (1969), who wanted to explain why the parents of someone described as an orphan could not be referred to using a definite pronoun, such as "them". Postal made the strong claim that pronouns could not take their meaning from parts of the meanings of words. However, other linguists suggested that cases in which a morphological relation existed between the pronoun's meaning and the preceding word ("him" = McCarthy, following "McCarthyites") were more acceptable. Browne's observation that a part–whole relation was not required between the anaphor's meaning and the antecedent's required substantial revisions both to the previous linguistic accounts of anaphoric islands and to processing theories that might be derived from them.

Only a small amount of research has been carried out on understanding references into anaphoric islands. Pronominal references into anaphoric islands are judged less acceptable than references in which the pronouns have ordinary noun phrase antecedents, and judgements about such sentences take longer to make. However, although this finding appears to suggest that an inference is necessary to understand a reference into an anaphoric island, this conclusion is compromised by the lack of an effect with noun phrase ante-cedents. Perhaps even when pronominal references into anaphoric islands are judged acceptable, their linguistically marginal nature interferes with the judgement. Other work, for example, with probe reaction times, is compatible with the idea that the referent of a pronoun that refers into an anaphoric island is readily available.

CHAPTER NINE

Implicit causality

Many texts, especially narratives, are about interrelated sequences of events that take place in the real, or an imaginary, world. Events have causes; people have reasons for their actions. The term *cause* is often used to refer to both causes and reasons. Indeed, there is a philosophical dispute about how, if at all, the two should be distinguished. In what follows the term will be used in this broad sense.

To understand a narrative properly it is necessary to compute the causal relations between the events described in it. Since one event can have several causes, and one cause several effects, the events in a narrative are often related to one another by complex *causal chains*. One set of questions about the comprehension of narratives centres around the computation of these causal chains (e.g., Fletcher & Bloom, 1988; Myers & Duffy, 1990; Trabasso & van den Broek, 1985; van den Broek & Trabasso, 1986). Interesting though these questions are, they have not typically been studied in relation to the central topic of this book—anaphora. That is not to say that computing such causal relations is irrelevant to resolving anaphors. Jerry Hobbs (1979) made the interesting suggestion that co-reference relations often fall out of the computation of coherence relations, and causal coherence is one of several types of coherence.

Asher and Lascarides (1998) endorse Hobbs's general position, but point out the need to distinguish between coherence based on discourse relations and coherence based on world knowledge. Coherence based on discourse relations must win out over world knowledge in establishing co-reference relations. For example in 9.1 "the rent" is the rent in John's new accommodation in St. John's Wood, even though it is well known (in the UK) that rents in St. John's Wood are higher than those in Brixton. The discourse is only coherent if the second sentence provides a reason for the first and, without other information, lower rents, not higher rents, provide reasons for moving.

(9.1)   John moved from Brixton to St. John's Wood.
        The rent was less expensive

This phenomenon reflects the fact that linguistic structure must take priority over plausible reasoning in determining meaning, otherwise it would not be possible to convey implausible messages.

LOCAL CAUSAL RELATIONS: IMPLICIT CAUSALITY

This chapter will consider local causal relations between two events, one the cause (or one of the causes) of the other. Co-reference between a pronoun in a clause describing one event and a name or full noun phrase in the clause describing the other is often established by computing coherence relations between the information in the two clauses. The aspect of causality that has been studied in relation to establishing such coherence relations, and hence the resolution of, in particular, definite pronouns, is *implicit causality*.

An event is said to have an implicit cause when the way it is described suggests, but does not explicitly state, how it was caused. More specifically, if an event is described using a particular verb, the cause of the event may be imputed to one participant in that event. Causes are often stated explicitly, as in 9.2

(9.2)   John went to the baker's. He wanted to buy some bread.

They may even be signalled linguistically, by a connective such as "because" in 9.3.

(9.3)   John went to the baker's, because he wanted to buy some bread.

Nevertheless, the cause of an event may remain implicit, particularly when it is not important to the development of a narrative. Even when a cause remains implicit, certain properties of the cause can often be guessed. However, although one event is usually regarded as causing another, it is only rarely that the precise event that is the implicit cause that can be guessed. For example, if an event is described by the clause "John blamed Bill", it is unlikely that a detailed guess about its cause (say, Bill was not paying attention as he carried the tea pot through a narrow doorway) will be correct. What may well be correct, however, is a guess about which participant in the event caused or precipitated it. For example, if John blamed Bill, other things being equal it is more likely that Bill did something wrong than that John was picking a fight.

Implicit causality and semantic roles

At an intuitive level, the two participants in an act of blaming can be thought of as the person doing the blaming ("the blamer") and a person being blamed ("the blamee"). More generally, it has been assumed that verbs have roles associated with them. These roles have been given various names such as deep cases (Fillmore, 1968) or, more recently, thematic roles (see papers in Wilkins, 1988). The nature of these thematic roles is a subject of debate (e.g., Ladusaw & Dowty, 1988). For this discussion, no particular view about these roles need be taken. In particular, it is not necessary to take the view that there is a small "universal" set of them (e.g., AGENT, THEME, GOAL, SOURCE, INSTRUMENT). Indeed, roles need only be identified for individual verbs (e.g., in an action of chasing, there is a chaser and a chasee, or person being chased).

Measuring implicit causality

The intuition that the blamee is likely to be the cause of an event of blaming can be operationalised using a sentence completion task. In this task, people are asked to provide an explicit cause for an event of which the cause is so far implicit. The linguistic signal for an explicit cause "because" is added to the end of a simple description, together (in one version) with a definite pronoun, as in 9.4.

   (9.4)   John blamed Bill because he . . .

The pronoun is intended to force the person completing the sentence to choose one of the two participants in the event of blaming as the main participant in the causing event. Here, the two participants in the main clause are of the same sex, so the pronoun can be interpreted as referring to either of them. Alternatively, the people can be given different sexes, and the pronoun omitted, as in 9.5.

   (9.5)   John blamed Jill because . . .

In this version the form of a pronoun, if one is produced, shows which character has been selected as the cause. A problem is that the completion may not refer to either character. Usually, however, the completion will make it obvious which character is taken to be the cause of the event. As stated earlier, with "blame", it is usual to choose the person being blamed, as in 9.6.

(9.6)   John blamed Bill because he left the knife in a dangerous place.

This person is the direct object of "blame" in a simple active sentence. For other verbs it is natural to choose the subject, as in 9.7.

(9.7)   John phoned Bill because he had to tell someone the news.

The choice of subject or object in such completions is only a bias. Acceptable sentences can be written in which the other participant in the event described by the main clause is chosen as the referent of the pronoun, as in 9.8 and 9.9.

(9.8)   John blamed Bill because he had to find a scapegoat.

(9.9)   John phoned Bill because he had asked to be told the outcome.

EMPIRICAL STUDIES OF IMPLICIT CAUSALITY

The phenomenon of implicit causality was first brought to the attention of linguists and psycholinguists by Garvey and Caramazza (1974). Those authors suggested that implicit causality was primarily associated with verbs, and using sentence completions they divided verbs into three categories: N1, N2, and NX. N1 verbs impute causality to the subject of a simple active clause (the first noun in that clause); N2 verbs impute causality to the object; NX verbs show no clear preference. Garvey and Caramazza placed the following verbs in these three categories:

N1:   confess, join, sell, telephone, chase, approach.
N2:   kill, fear, criticise, blame, punish, scold, praise, congratulate, admire.
NX: help, recognise, give, argue with, miss

In later writings, and in recognition of the fact that noun phrases rather than nouns refer to participants in events, the labels N1 and N2 were changed to NP1 and NP2, and this terminology will be used henceforth.

Garvey and Caramazza also suggested that factors other than the meaning of the verb could "influence or attenuate" (1974, p. 462) the bias of a verb. The factors that they identified included: negation, the relative social status of the participants, and the informational structure of the sentence. So, "John blamed Bill because he . . ." is likely to produce more NP2 completions than "John did not blame Bill because he . . .", and "The father blamed his son because he . . ." is likely to produce more NP2 completions than "The son blamed his father because he . . .". Changing the information structure, for example by passivising the main clause, has more complex effects. The general tendency of passivisation, however, is to shift the choice of antecedent to the surface subject (see Caramazza & Gupta, 1979).

The sentence completion data alluded to by Garvey and Caramazza (1974) were presented in more detail by Garvey, Caramazza, and Yates (1975), who also considered whether implicit causality should be analysed in terms of a more fundamental semantic feature of verbs. Since causality is imputed to a participant in an event, and since participants fulfil roles, a natural suggestion is that implicit causality may be explained by the underlying roles of the participants. Fillmore's (1968) theory of case grammar was influential at the time this work was carried out, but Garvey et al. argued that implicit causality cannot be explained by cases, for two reasons. First, the effects of social status (a boss arguing with an assistant versus an assistant arguing with a boss) cannot be explained by case relations. Second, the effects of passivisation cannot be so explained, either. Neither social status nor passivization affects those relations, but both affect imputed causes.

In a later paper, Grober et al. (1978) argued that the use of implicit causality to assign referents to pronouns was itself a modulation of a more basic *parallel function strategy* (see Chapter 6) in which the role of a pronoun in its clause is assumed to be the same as the role of the antecedent in its clause. In a fragment such as 9.10, "he" is the subject of the second clause.

(9.10)   John blamed Bill . . . he . . .

"John" plays the parallel role in the first clause, so the preferred assignment is for "he" to be linked with John. If the connective "because" is replaced by "but", which does not signal a causal relation, sentence completions almost always follow the predictions of the parallel function hypothesis in Grober et al.'s data. However, their task does not distinguish between a preference for parallel function and a preference for antecedents in subject position, since the pronouns themselves were always in subject position in their clause (see, e.g., Stevenson et al., 1995 for a discussion of the relation between parallel function and subject assignment).

Grober et al. (1978) also report effects of the inclusion of modal verbs. When the protagonists were introduced by proper names, strong modals, such as "must", strengthened the imputation of cause by the main verb. Weak modals, such as "may", allowed implicit causality to be overridden by parallel function. So, for example, in 9.11 the scolding most likely takes place because of something Mark has done, given that Alexander has been introduced by his name and not by a(n authority) role.

(9.11)   Alexander must scold Mark.

However, in 9.12 it is likely to be something about Nancy that determines whether the scolding takes place.

(9.12)   Nancy may scold Marge.

Roles revisited

Although Garvey et al. (1975) considered, and rejected, the idea of explaining implicit causality using Fillmorean deep cases, similar ideas have subsequently been reconsidered. In particular, Brown and Fish (1983) suggested an analysis of implicit causality based on verb types and what they called the *semantic roles* of the arguments of a verb. They argued that action verbs impute causes to their agents, rather than their patients, and that mental state verbs impute causes to their stimuli, rather than to the person experiencing the mental state (the experiencer). On this view, action verbs impute the cause to their subject (in active sentences), but mental state verbs may impute the cause to either the subject or the object, because some of these verbs (e.g., "amaze") have the stimulus as subject and others (e.g., "admire") have the experiencer as subject. In support of this view, Brown and Fish consider adjectives derived from verbs. They argue that either the only or the most common adjective attributes a property to the cause imputed by the verb. So, "admire" yields "admirable" (with "admiring" being less common as an attributive adjective) and "amaze" yields "amazing" (not "amazable").

However, not only do Brown and Fish (1983) fail to counter Garvey et al.'s (1975) arguments against an analysis using cases, their claims are not consistent with the original data of Garvey et al. As Au (1986) points out, some action verbs impute causation to the patient, not the agent. For example, "punish" is both an action verb and one than imputes causality to NP2. Au suggests several factors that may affect attributions of causality with action verbs. For verbs of judging ("praise", "blame", "scold", "criticise", etc.), he invokes Fillmore's (1971) notion of *presupposed responsibility*. For other action verbs (e.g., "sell", "telephone", "kill"), he suggests two, not necessarily independent, factors: intention, and Osgood's (1970) distinction between initiating and reacting participants in an event. Au, following Fillenbaum and Rapoport (1971, 1974) also performed multidimensional scaling on similarity judgements for actions verbs. This analysis produced two dimensions, which Au identified as good versus bad and cause imputed to agent versus cause imputed to patient. Au follows Fillmore (1977) in suggesting that the imputed cause depends on the *scenes* that a verb brings to mind, and notes that this view is compatible with Johnson-Laird's (1983) theory of mental models of discourse.

An alternative view (Crinean & Garnham, 1999) is that those action verbs that show NP2 causality (e.g., "thank", "accuse") have an experiencer–

stimulus component to their meaning. So, although punishing requires the carrying out of an action, punishment is typically prompted by a reaction of the agent who will perform the action to some aspect of or action by the person who will be punished, and who therefore acts in a role similar to the stimulus in a pure stimulus–experiencer verb in which the response is purely psychological.

Implicit causality and attribution theory

Both Au (1986) and Brown and Fish (1983) point out the link between the implicit causality of verbs and the attribution of causes studied in social psychology under the head of attribution theory (Heider, 1958; Jones & Davies, 1965; Kelley, 1967). Traditionally, studies of attribution use language merely as a vehicle for presenting information about events for people to make judgements about. More recently, and partly in response to the research of Au and of Brown and Fish, some attribution theorists have suggested a more prominent role for language in the attribution process (e.g., Semin & Fiedler, 1989), whereas others have resisted this move (e.g., Edwards & Potter, 1993), claiming that particular attributions rely heavily on contextual factors that are not, and typically cannot be, encoded semantically.

From a (psycho)linguistic point of view, the work of Au and of Brown and Fish can be taken as a first step in attempting to determine what underlies imputations of causality. They have identified one clear pattern: With mental states, the person or object that induces the mental state (the stimulus) is taken as the cause, not the person who has the mental state (the experiencer). The real world fact that underlies this observation is that people do not generally induce particular mental states in themselves, particularly mental states that are directed towards other people. Someone may cultivate a taste for oysters, but once they have that taste, eating oysters becomes a pleasurable experience. For actions the pattern is less clear, and is complicated by whether the underlying semantics of the verb make the action a response to the person acted on.

From the same (psycholinguistic) perspective, the conclusions reached by Edwards and Potter merely underline the fact that imputations of cause can be overridden by other factors. As mentioned previously, this point was recognised by Garvey and Caramazza (1974). For example, Edwards and Potter consider the verb "telephone" which, in Au's (1986) data was consistently rated as an NP1 verb (agent causal). As Edwards and Potter point out, Betty's telephoning of John may be explained by the fact that John left a message on Betty's answering machine. Despite, its status as a strong NP1 verb, "telephone" can occur in a sentence such as 9.13.

(9.13)   Betty telephoned John because he left a message on the answering machine.

Furthermore, even in 9.14 it is clear that "she" is intended to refer to Jean.

> (9.14)   Betty telephoned Jean because she left a message on the answering machine.

Consistency between implicit and explicit causes

The previous example illustrates a fact mentioned before: An explicitly stated cause may either be consistent with an implicit cause or be inconsistent with it. In the inconsistent case, the explicit cause takes precedence. If implicit causality plays a role in comprehension, it would be expected that an explicit cause following an implicit one, but inconsistent with it, would be more difficult to understand than a(n otherwise comparable) explicit clause that was consistent with the implicit cause. Garvey and Caramazza ended their 1974 article with this suggestion and, in further work (Caramazza et al., 1977), provided empirical evidence in support of it. Caramazza et al. presented sentences such as 9.15 and 9.16.

> (9.15)   Tom scolded Bill because he was annoying.
> (NP2 verb, so ending is consistent with implicit causality)

> (9.16)   Tom scolded Bill because he was annoyed.
> (ending is inconsistent with implicit causality)

People had to read the sentences and to say out loud the name of the person that the pronoun referred to. There were also versions of the sentences in which the pronoun could be resolved by gender, such as 9.17 and 9.18.

> (9.17)   Sue scolded Bill because he was annoying.

> (9.18)   Tom scolded Sue because he was annoyed.

Although people were quicker to read the sentences and say the name of the pronoun when there was a gender cue, the effect of implicit causality (quicker responding when the ending was consistent than when it was inconsistent) was present for sentences with and without a gender cue to the identity of the pronoun's referent. Indeed, and perhaps surprisingly, the effect of implicit causality was numerically larger when there was a gender cue (320 ms versus 136 ms). Vonk (1985b) reported a similar pattern of results: main effects of gender cue and consistency (which she called congruence) and no interaction. However, when she changed the task from pronoun naming to sentence verification, so that the reading time for the pronoun containing clause could be measured separately, she found reliable effects of consistency on sentence reading time, but no effect of gender cueing. The time taken to verify the subsequently presented test item did, however, show effects both of gender cue and of consistency. Vonk (1984) separated reading and naming effects in a different way: by monitoring people's eye movements while they read the sentences, but before they named the pronouns. In this study only sentences with consistent endings were used, so effects of consistency could not be studied. There was no overall effect of gender cueing, but people spent longer looking at the pronoun, and less time looking at the rest of the second clause, when there was a gender cue. Vonk (1985a) monitored eye movements in a study in which the task was sentence verification. In this study the only significant effect in reading was that of consistency on the last part of the second clause. There were no effects of gender cue, neither overall, nor in the separate parts of the sentences.

Vonk argued that the naming task focuses attention on pronoun resolution, and hence on the relevance of the pronouns' gender. However, her verification experiments included filler items with no pronouns. Furthermore, the verification statements for the experimental items did not always require pronoun resolution. So, the relevance of the pronouns' gender differed considerably across Vonk's two tasks.

The idea that gender information can be used in a task-specific way is consistent with the findings of Garnham et al. (1992), who were attempting to resolve the discrepancy between Vonk's findings and those of Garnham and Oakhill (1985). Garnham and Oakhill carried out a self-paced reading experiment in which sentences such as 9.19 were read.

(9.19)   Vicky/Alan lent a pen to Jill, because she wanted to write a letter.

After each sentence a simple yes/no question was presented that required resolution of the pronoun, for example 9.20.

(9.20)   Did Vicky/Alan want to write a letter?

In this study there was a clear effect of gender cue. However, in a post hoc analysis, the effect of the consistency of the ending of the sentence with the bias of the verb was restricted to sentences in which there was also a gender cue. As noted earlier, Caramazza et al. had found a numerically larger effect of consistency when it was paired with gender cueing.

The pronoun naming task produces reliable effects of both gender cueing and consistency (Caramazza et al., 1977; Vonk, 1985b). However, the task is clearly an artificial one. Vonk's findings with the verification task suggest that gender cueing may be unimportant in reading itself. However, since gender (in English) can be such an obvious cue to the referent of a pronoun, it is surprising that people are not normally helped in understanding a pronoun when only one of its possible referents matches it in gender. In Dutch (the language of Vonk's experiments), matters are somewhat more complex since "zij" is ambiguous between third-person feminine singular ("she") and third-person plural ("they"), so there is an additional, if temporary, ambiguity in a Dutch sentence that begins as in 9.21.

(9.21)   Antje . . . Judith omdat zij . . .
Annie . . . Judith because she (or they) . . .

It was not, therefore, obvious that the finding (Garnham & Oakhill, 1985) of a gender cueing effect in English had a strategic explanation. Nor was the failure to find reliable consistency effects entirely satisfactory, since that variable was identified post hoc, and there was not a good balance of NP1 and NP2 verbs.

Garnham et al. (1992) report two series of experiments. The first was based on the observation that the inferences required to resolve the pronouns in Vonk's no cue conditions were simple. For example, the English translation of one of her materials is 9.22.

(9.22)   Harry won the money from Albert because he played skilfully.

In Garnham and Oakhill's materials more complex inferences were often required, as for example in 9.23.

(9.23)   Julie blamed Trudy because she had discovered some relevant evidence.

Implicit causality contributes to the inference making process, but that process has other components. So the simpler the inference the clearer the effects of causality should be. Gender cueing, on the other hand, provides a method of by-passing the inference and resolving the pronoun in a different way. It should, therefore, have a greater effect when it is helping to by-pass a more complex inference. Thus, Vonk's materials, with their simple inferences, may have accentuated the role of implicit causality and masked the role of gender cueing, whereas Garnham and Oakhill's materials, with their complex inferences, may have had the opposite effects. This idea was tested in three experiments, with two sets of materials used in all three experiments, in which the complexity of the inferences was systematically varied. The experiments produced a mixed picture of cueing and consistency effects. However, whenever either cueing or consistency interacted with complexity of inference, *both* had larger effects in the sentences with simple inferences. These results are consistent with the idea that implicit causality contributes to the inference process. It would have been surprising if they had not been. However, they are not consistent with the idea that gender cueing was masked in Vonk's experiments by the simplicity of the inferences that provided an alternative route to resolving the pronoun.

A second set of experiments (Garnham et al., 1992, Exps. 4 and 5) investigated the possibility that the effects of gender cue were under strategic control. In the first of these experiments experimental items of the kind used before were mixed either with more items of the same kind or with other items that had similar main verbs, but no pronoun in the "because" clause, for example 9.24 and 9.25.

(9.24)   Roger questioned Trisha because the previous suspect had been cleared.

(9.25)   Vicky lied to Alan because the truth was too dreadful.

Each sentence was followed by a yes/no question, which, for the experimental sentences, required resolution of the pronoun.

In this experiment there were clear effects of consistency on the reading times for the second clauses of the sentences, but the effect of gender cueing was confined to the condition in which the filler items also contained pronouns that had to be resolved to answer the questions. The effect of cueing reappeared in the question-answering times.

In the final experiment the crucial sentences were inserted into passages such as 9.26.

(9.26)   Alan was trying to choose
          a summer holiday for his family.
          Brian, his brother,
          worked for a travel agency.
          Alan phoned Brian because
          he needed to get some information.
          It was soon decided that
          the family would spend a fortnight in Corfu.
          All the brochures promised
          exceptionally good weather.

          Were the family going on holiday in winter?
          Did Alan need to get some information?
          Do you think hot sun is a very important part of a holiday?

As this example shows, there were three questions after each passage. One required resolution of the pronoun, but the final question was always a more interesting one, that required a value judgement. Comments made after the experiment showed that people thought this question was the most important.

The results of this experiment also showed a clear effect of implicit causality on the reading time for the second clause of the crucial sentence, but no effect of gender cue. Again the effect of gender cue reappeared in the answering time for the relevant question (the middle one). Furthermore, in this experiment, because of the intervening material, this gender cueing effect could not be attributed to spillover. The likely explanation of the effect is, therefore, that in the mental model of a passage two people of the same sex are less distinctly represented than two people of different sexes. It is therefore easier to answer a "who did what" question in the latter case.

These results clearly show that the use of gender cue information to speed comprehension is under strategic control. It does not follow, however, that people ignore gender information when it is not speeding their comprehension. For example, it is likely that they would baulk if a main clause with two male names was followed by a subordinate clause with the pronoun "she". Nevertheless, in circumstances that approach those of normal reading, the presence or absence of a gender cue does not affect how long is needed to interpret a pronoun-containing clause.

A series of experiments by McKoon, Greene and Ratcliff (1993) suggest that implicit causality has little effect on comprehension when there is also a gender cue to the referent of a pronoun. They presented sentences such as 9.27–9.30 as the last sentences of brief texts.

(9.27)   James infuriated Debbie because he leaked important information to the press.

(9.28)   James infuriated Debbie because she had to write all the speeches.

(9.29)   Diane valued Sam because he always knew how to negotiate.

(9.30)   Diane valued Sam because she never knew how to negotiate.

The verb "infuriate" is an NP1 verb while "value" is an NP2 verb (McKoon, Greene, & Ratcliff use the terms *subject initiating* and *object initiating*). The endings of 9.27 and 9.29 are consistent with the implicit causality of the verb in the first clause, and the endings of 9.28 and 9.30 are inconsistent. The first and third sentences should, therefore, be easier to understand than the second and fourth.

McKoon, Greene, and Ratcliff (1993) used a probe word task, with probes at the end of the sentences. They tested NP1 verbs (Exps. 1 and 2) and NP2 verbs (Exps. 3 and 4), with normal (Exps. 1 and 3) or speeded (Exps. 2 and 4) response instructions. In all four experiments there was an interaction between the character name (subject or object of the first clause) and whether the second clause was consistent or inconsistent with the implicit causality of the verb in the first clause. This interaction represents faster responding to the *referent* of the pronoun as opposed to the *non-referent* (see McKoon, Greene,

& Ratcliff 1993, p. 1045), an effect that is independent of implicit causality (either verb bias or consistency of ending).

Effects of implicit causality could have shown up in two ways in these experiments. First, proactive highlighting of one participant using the bias of the verb would produce a main effect of character name on probe reaction time or probe errors. Since NP1 and NP2 verbs were tested in different experiments, the subject test name would be favoured in the NP1 verb experiments, and the object test name in the NP2 experiments. Second, if consistent endings are easier to understand than inconsistent ones, responding to the probe name might suffer more interference from understanding the sentence (or vice versa) for inconsistent endings. Such interference could produce a main effect of consistency on either probe reaction time or probe errors (if comprehension interferes with the probe task), or a main effect of the same variable on responses in the verification task that followed each passage (if the probe task interferes with comprehension). Of all these possible effects of implicit causality, only two were significant over the set of four experiments. In Experiment 2 there was an effect of test character on probe reaction time, and in Experiment 3 there was an effect of test character on errors in responding to the probes. In other words, effects of implicit causality were weak and inconsistent compared to the clear referent/non-referent effect. Indeed, McKoon, Greene, and Ratcliff's claim that verbs that show implicit causality "make the initiator relatively more accessible in a comprehender's discourse model and that this change in accessibility aids identification of the referent of a pronoun in a following 'because' clause" (1993, abstract, see also p. 1049) is hardly justified by their findings.

McKoon, Greene, and Ratcliff's results appear to conflict with the findings reported earlier that implicit causality effects tend to be stronger when there is also a gender cue. However, they did not compare cue and no-cue conditions. Furthermore, given the complex inferences needed to link the information in the two clauses of the sentences they used, their results are consistent with previous findings on implicit causality (see Garnham et al., 1992, for a brief overview). The clearest effects of implicit causality have been found when the inferential links between the clause with the implicitly causal verb and the following "because" clause are simple (Vonk, 1984, 1985a, b versus Garnham & Oakhill, 1985).

Early versus late effects implicit causality

In discussing the results of McKoon, Greene, and Ratcliff (1993) the idea of early versus late effects was mentioned. The notion of early and late effects was developed by Garnham, Traxler, Oakhill, and Gernsbacher (1996), who distinguished between effects of implicit causality on focusing and effects on integration. Focusing is an effect of the bias of the verb (whether it is NP1 or

NP2). In a focusing account, the verb that imputes causality immediately *highlights* one participant (for example James in 9.27 and 9.28, Sam in 9.29 and 9.30 and makes it a stronger candidate than other participants for later pronominal reference. This idea is consistent with McKoon, Greene, and Ratcliff's theoretical position. It is not, however supported by their findings.

Basing their account on *centering theory* (Grosz et al., 1995), McKoon, Greene, and Ratcliff claim that a pronoun is only readily interpreted when there is just one candidate for its reference. Focusing using implicit causality would provide such a referent, and could explain why they found evidence for immediate pronoun resolution, when Greene, et al. (1992), who used sentences such as 9.31 with verbs that did not impute causality, did not.

(9.31)   Mary accidentally scratched John with a knife and then she dropped it on the counter.

As mentioned in the discussion of McKoon, Greene, and Ratcliff (1993), implicit causality effects could arise at various points in reading a typical two clause sentence such as 9.32.

(9.32)   Max confessed to Bill because he wanted a reduced sentence.

Experiments in which a global measure, such as clause reading time, is taken make it difficult to determine the locus of the effect. McKoon, Greene, and Ratcliff used a probe word technique, but only presented probe words at the end of the sentence. By using probe words within the sentence, more information about the locus of the effect can be obtained.

Garnham et al. (1996) used this technique to distinguish between a focusing, or proactive, account of implicit causality and an integrative, or retroactive, account. Focusing effects should be detectable at the end of the clause in which the action was described, and might be discernible earlier, particularly if the implicit cause is the sentential subject. The increased prominence given to the implicit clause should make it easier to identify it as the referent of a following pronoun than to so identify another participant in the same action. A retroactive account would claim that implicit causality only has an effect when information about an explicit cause (in the "because" clause) is linked with information about the event it causes (described in the main clause of the sentences typically used in these experiments).

Garnham et al. (1996) found no evidence for focusing effects. In their first three experiments, where no gender cueing was available, there was an effect of consistency (whether the implicit and explicit causes were the same) which was found primarily at the end of the "because" clause, supporting an integration account. In the fourth experiment, in which gender cueing was provided, there was still no focusing effect of the bias of the verb, but there was evidence that the pronoun's referent was determined just after the pronoun had been read, presumably on the basis of gender cueing, as in the McKoon, Greene, and Ratcliff (1993) study. Stewart, Pickering, and Sanford (2000) provide further evidence for the integration account, using self-paced reading techniques.

Although Garnham et al. (1996) found no evidence for focusing, a study by McDonald and MacWhinney (1995) did report such effects. McDonald and MacWhinney used a cross-modal priming technique (auditory presentation of sentences, visual presentation of probes). They found effects of verb bias (NP1 versus NP2) immediately following the pronoun, both with and without a gender cue to the referent of the pronoun. However, in the sentences used by McDonald and MacWhinney the implicit and explicit causes were always the same—there were no inconsistent endings. The bias of the verb in the main clause was, therefore, a reliable cue to the referent of the pronoun. Later studies by McDonald (1997) have suggested that the use of verb bias information is under strategic control. When it is a reliable cue to the referent of a pronoun it is used, as in the original McDonald and MacWhinney experiments, but when it has no predictive value, because half of the following "because" clauses have endings that are consistent with the implicit cause and half have endings that are inconsistent, it is not used. McDonald also showed, as Garnham et al. (1992) had, that the use of gender cue information is under strategic control.

Oakhill, Garnham, Reynolds, and Wilshire (1998) suggest that the effects of implicit causality on reading may not be integrative effects, but effects arising at a lower level of processing. In a typical implicit causality experiment, different "because" clauses provide consistent and inconsistent continuations from the same main clause. Oakhill et al. used the same "because" clauses as consistent and inconsistent continuations of different main clauses, as in 9.33 and 9.34

(9.33)   John appreciated Ian because he was a good worker.

(9.34)   Paul missed Ron because he was a good worker.

In self-paced reading experiments, Oakhill et al. found no implicit causality effect on reading times for the "because" clauses, despite using at least as many people and sentences as in studies where clear effects had been reported. Furthermore, they continued to find consistency effects on other measures, such as time taken to answer comprehension questions, and percentage of positive judgements about whether the "because" clause was a sensible continuation from the main clause.

IMPLICIT CONSEQUENTIALITY

Just as events have causes, they have consequences. Indeed, Moens and Steedman (1988) suggest that actions, but not states, have a tripartite representation, comprising precondition, body, and consequences. Stevenson, Crawley, and Kleinman (1994) suggested that in a narrative text attention naturally shifts to the consequences of the event currently being described. From this point of view, later mention of the cause is a marked case, a fact consistent with the finding that implicit causality biases can disappear if the connective "because" is changed to a different one, for example "and" or "but" (Ehrlich, 1980). Stevenson et al. (1994, Exp. 3) showed that when people completed a sentence fragment ending with "so", as in 9.35a, they tended to refer to the consequences of the main event, whereas in 9.35b they tended to refer to the cause.

(9.35a)   Joseph hit Patrick, so . . .
(9.35b)   Joseph hit Patrick, because . . .

Furthermore, pronominal reference tended to be to different characters in the two cases.

In an attempt to explain these results, Stevenson et al. (1994) returned to the idea first suggested by Garvey and Caramazza (1974), though rejected by them, that implicit causality effects can be explained using roles. Stevenson et al.'s analysis makes use of thematic roles, a more recent counterpart to Fillmorean cases. Stevenson et al. argue that the shift associated with the change from "so" to "because" occurs because different thematic roles are associated with the cause and the consequence of an event. In the case of an action, as in 9.35, the agent is seen as causing the event that has consequences primarily for the patient.

Stewart, Pickering, and Sanford (1998a) suggested that, just as a verb can exhibit implicit causality, it might also show *implicit consequentiality*. So, in the absence of information to the contrary, the consequences of the action may be seen as arising primarily for a particular participant in the event. Stewart et al. measured implicit causality in a sentence completion study, using fragments such as 9.36.

(9.36)   Because Sue dreaded John, . . .

Of the 50 verbs tested, 16 showed strong implicit consequentiality effects. Stewart, Pickering, and Sanford (1998b) claimed that there was no obvious relation between a verb's implicit causality and its implicit consequentiality. However, Crinean and Garnham (1999) have showed that, for stimulus–experiencer verbs and for NP1 action verbs the implicit cause and the implicit consequence differ. For NP2 action verbs, which they argue have an experiencer–stimulus component to their meaning (see earlier), the implicit cause and the implicit consequence are the same. This idea is consistent with data on consequentiality reported by Au (1986), who showed that the consequences of an event are associated with the experiencer for stimulus–experiencer verbs and the patient for agent–patient verbs.

SUMMARY

The notion of implicit causality was introduced by Garvey and Caramazza (1974). They suggested that the use of a particular verb could suggest which participant in an event had (probably) caused it to happen. They identified several factors that could modulate implicit causality, and suggested that it could not be explained, or at least not wholly explained, using the semantic roles associated with the verb.

Empirical studies have shown that implicit causality can be measured using sentence completion tasks, and that it can have effects on reading times and other measures associated with processing an explicit cause that is either the same as (consistent with) or different from (inconsistent with) the implicit cause. Inconsistency typically slows responses. These studies have also confirmed many of Garvey and Caramazza's suggestions about factors that modulate implicit causality.

Brown and Fish (1983) argued that semantic roles do have a central place in explaining implicit causality, and identified two main patterns one for state verbs (stimulus as cause) and one for action verbs (agent as cause). However, their claim about action verbs failed to allow for action verbs that impute causality to the person acted upon. Such verbs, which were among those originally described by Garvey and Caramazza, also show an atypical relation between their implicit causes and their implicit consequences.

There is some evidence that the use of implicit causality information is under strategic control. When it is not reliable (i.e., when many instances of inconsistency are encountered), implicit causality information appears to be used late in the comprehension process, and it may even be that, under such circumstances, reading time effects are an artefact of the different materials used in the consistent and inconsistent sentences.

CHAPTER TEN

Stereotypes

In many texts the main protagonists represented in mental models are people. People may be introduced by a variety of means, of which the most common are proper names and full definite noun phrases. Such expressions, together with demonstratives, pronouns, and zero anaphors may also be used for later references to the same person. Many names are conventionally used for people of a particular sex. For example, Susan is a name for females, and will only be applied to males under exceptional circumstances. A reference to a person named Susan, unless it is accompanied by a specific comment about the sex of the person it refers to, can be taken as a reference to a female, and that person can be represented in the corresponding mental model as a female.

Some nouns are defined by the sex of the people they can refer to, most obviously nouns such as "man" and "woman". So, if a definite noun phrase anaphor is based on one of these nouns, technically if it has such a noun as its head, the sex of the person that the noun phrase refers to will be determined by the gender of the noun. This property of the noun phrase holds both when the noun phrase is simple ("the man") and when it is more complex ("the man we saw juggling in the street when we went on the day trip to Burnsall on last year's holiday").

Not all references to people provide such information about sex. Many nouns, for example "child" or "parent", can refer to both males and females. However, there are many ways of specifying people's sex when it is necessary to do so. There may be alternative, more specific, nouns ("boy", "girl", "mother", "father"). Adjectives may make sex clear ("bearded", "pregnant"), as may following pronouns or possessives ("he", "she", "him", "her", "his", "hers"). There is, however, a set of nouns that, while not specifying the sex of the person that they apply to as part of their meaning, more commonly apply to people of one sex than the other, nouns such as "nurse" and "engineer". Such nouns can be referred to as *stereotyped*, though this label need imply no more than that (people believe) there are more female nurses than male nurses and more male engineers than female engineers. There can be more to stereotyping: beliefs about what jobs or roles are appropriate for males and females, for example. However, such beliefs are not directly relevant to the issues under study here.

If a person called Susan is represented in a mental model as female, and a person described as an aunt is represented as female, how is a person described as a nurse represented? Nurses may be stereotypically female, but being a nurse is not defined by the sex of the person doing the job. Furthermore, the existence of male nurses is well known. A nurse could be represented as probably female, female unless there is information to the contrary, or a nurse's sex might not be represented at all.

There are many informal reports of experiments on stereotyping. All claim to show that, when a person is introduced into a text using a noun phrase based on a stereotyped noun such as "typist", a following clause containing a pronoun that matches the stereotype is read more quickly than one in which the pronoun does not match the stereotype. There are now also a few published studies showing this effect (e.g., Carreiras, Garnham, Oakhill, & Cain, 1996; Kerr & Underwood, 1984). Carreiras et al. (1996, Exp. 1) presented passages such as 10.1a followed by 10.1b or 10.1c.

(10.1a)   The electrician examined the light fitting.
(10.1b)   He needed a special attachment to fix it.
(10.1c)   She needed a special attachment to fix it.

They found that 10.1c was read more slowly than 10.1b. This result appears to support the idea that an electrician is represented as male, or at least probably male. On this view, the mismatch between the represented maleness of the electrician and the feminine morphology of "she" in 10.1c slows readers down. However, it is possible that the sex of the electrician is only considered when the pronoun is encountered, and that the information about the usual sex of electricians only becomes available at that point.

Carreiras et al. (1996, Exps. 2–4) showed that a similar effect arose earlier in Spanish, in which a noun such as "cantante" (singer) combines with either a masculine ("el") or feminine ("la") definite article to form a noun phrase. So, 10.2a (translation 10.3a) was read more quickly than 10.2b (translation 10.3b). However, once it had been established that the nurse was male in

10.2b, no further difficulty was encountered. 10.2e (translation 10.3e) was read just as quickly as 10.2d (translation 10.3d).

(10.2a) La enfermera tuvo que suturar la herida.
(10.2b) El enfermero tuvo que suturar la herida.
(10.2c) El corte había sido profundo.
(10.2d) Ella también puso una inyección para eviatar una infección.
(10.2e) El también puso una inyección para eviatar una infección.

(10.3a) The (female) nurse had to suture the injury.
(10.3b) The (male) nurse had to suture the injury.
(10.3c) It had been a deep cut.
(10.3d) She also gave an injection to avoid an infection.
(10.3e) He also gave an injection to avoid an infection.

Duffy and Keir (1998) reported a similar result in English, in an eye-tracking experiment. With no preceding information, readers slow down on 10.4a compared with 10.4b.

(10.4a) The electrician taught herself . . .
(10.4b) The electrician taught himself . . .

However, when previous context had established the sex of the electrician, this effect disappeared.

The early effect in Spanish reported by Carreiras et al. (1996) and the equivalent effect in English reported by Duffy and Keir lend further weight to the argument that people referred to by stereotyped nouns are represented as having, or probably having, a particular sex. However, the argument is still not conclusive, since in both sets of studies the information in the stereotyped noun had to be put together with other information (the gender of the definite article in Spanish, and the explicit statement about the sex of the person in Duffy and Keir's experiment). It could be that the gender information associated with stereotyped nouns is only accessed by such combinatory processes.

Reynolds, Garnham, and Oakhill (2000) suggested a different approach, using a pencil-and-paper task, based on a riddle whose relevance to questions about inferencing had been pointed out by Sanford (1985b, 1987). Reynolds et al. (2000) used the modified version of the riddle shown in 10.5.

(10.5) This morning a father and his son were driving along the motor-way to work, when they were involved in a horrible accident. The father was killed and the son was quickly driven to hospital severely injured. When the boy was taken into the hospital a passing surgeon exclaimed: "Oh my God, that is my son!"

This modified version allowed the construction of minimally different versions with a non-stereotyped term ("physiotherapist", ending 10.6) and a gender-marked term ("fireman", ending 10.7):

(10.6) When the boy was taken into the hospital a passing physiotherapist exclaimed: "Oh my God, that is my son!"

(10.7) When the boy was taken into the hospital a passing fireman exclaimed: "Oh my God, that is my son!"

Reynolds et al. reasoned that if people do not initially take the surgeon to be male, they should not experience difficulties with the passage, as all the other information in it points to the surgeon being the boy's mother. The strong constraint that the boy's father is dead, and cannot be the surgeon, should override the weaker constraint that surgeons are typically male (but can also be female), and lead to the conclusion that the surgeon is the boy's mother. Only if readers commit themselves to the maleness of the surgeon before they encounter the other constraints (that the boy is the surgeon's son, which reinstates the relevance of the boy's father being dead) will they be unable to derive a consistent interpretation of the passage. Many people were not able to derive this interpretation until it was pointed out to them, suggesting that a person described as a surgeon is initially represented as being male. Of those who did solve the riddle, a substantial proportion reported having seen similar puzzles before.

This interpretation of the findings is supported by the results from another version of the passage. In this version the information that a person in the hospital claimed to be the boy's mother was presented before the information that that person was a surgeon, so that the final sentence was 10.8.

(10.8) "Oh my God, that is my son!" was heard from a passing surgeon when the boy was taken into the hospital.

In this version about three-quarters of the readers came to the correct interpretation with little difficulty, suggesting that the order of presentation of the information determines which constraints on interpretation take priority.

In a further attempt to provide evidence that the likely sex of characters described using role names cannot be suppressed, Oakhill, Garnham, and Reynolds (2000b) carried out an experiment in which people were asked to judge whether two terms, such as "nurse" and "brother", could apply to the same individual. The question was deliberately phrased as one of possibilities, rather than probabilities. On the crucial trials the first term was a role name and the second term was a kinship term that had a particular sex as part of its meaning (a brother must be male). The results were that, although people were usually correct, they were slower and made more errors when the stereotype associated with the role name mismatched the sex of the kinship term (e.g., "nurse", "uncle", or "engineer", "mother"). In follow-up studies people were given more time to consider the role name, and in one experiment specific instructions informing them that they should not be misled by stereotypes. However, an incongruity effect still emerged. It also emerged in an experiment in which speeded responding was required. So whether people are hurried, working at their own pace, or have more than enough time to consider the role name, incongruity effects occur. Interestingly, congruity with the stereotype never speeded responding compared with a neutral condition, in which the role names were not stereotyped (as rated by Carreiras et al., 1996). Indeed, in some experiments responses to neutral items (e.g., "student", "mother") were quicker than those to items in which the stereotype was congruent with the gender of the kinship term. This result suggests that processing of gender information may have been occurring for the congruent pairs, even though it was not necessary to make the correct judgement that the terms could apply to the same individual.

Similar results have been reported by Banaji and Hardin (1996). They asked people to classify pronouns as masculine or feminine (1996, Exp. 1) or to classify a mixture of words as pronouns or non-pronouns (1996, Exp. 2). In both experiments the pronouns followed a variety of gender-related words, including stereotyped role names, and in both experiments judgements were speeded when the gender of the pronoun matched that of the stereotype.

SUMMARY

Facts about the world determine that someone referred to as a beautician is probably female, whereas someone referred to as a judge is probably male. However, it is not part of the meaning of "beautician" or "judge" that people who fill these roles are of a particular sex. Nevertheless, there is converging evidence that the sexes of people described by stereotyped role names are encoded into mental models. What is not completely clear, on the basis of the evidence to date, is whether a nurse is represented as being definitely female, in the absence of information to the contrary, or merely very likely female. In either case, inferences about the gender or probable gender of characters described by role names may be one of the few cases in which forward inference are made in comprehension.

CHAPTER ELEVEN

A mental models theory of understanding anaphora

This book has outlined the theory of mental models, as applied to language processing, and has presented a wide range of linguistic and psycholinguistic ideas about anaphoric expressions and their interpretation. This final chapter briefly reviews some of the main themes that have emerged in the quest for a theory of anaphor interpretation.

MENTAL MODELS AS REPRESENTATIONS OF TEXT CONTENT

According to the mental models theory, texts are represented in mental models of the situations they are about. Those situations may be situations in the real world, situations in a fictional world, or situations in a world of abstract ideas. Situations comprise individuals (or abstract ideas), their properties, and the relations between them. Thus mental models must contain representations of those individuals, ideas, properties, and relations. A mental models theory of comprehension must explain how representations of particular individuals, ideas, properties, and relations get into the model of a particular text. Individuals may be explicitly mentioned (typically using noun phrases) or inferred. Properties are denoted by modifiers. Relations may be conveyed directly, for example by verbs, or indirectly, for example, for temporal relations, by relations between verb forms (tense and aspect) in different clauses. Anaphoric expressions may refer to things already represented in the model, or closely related to them. A theory of anaphor comprehension must explain how an expression is identified as anaphoric, or potentially ana-phoric, and how it is assigned a meaning when it has been so identified. Chapter 6 discussed these issues in some depth.

MENTAL MODELS AND REPRESENTATIONS OF SURFACE FORM

Although mental models theory focuses on representations of situations, it is a well-established psycholinguistic fact that people represent other aspects of a text in addition to its information content. In particular, various aspects of the superficial form of texts are encoded. Although there is a connection, pointed out by Hankamer and Sag (1976), between two classes of anaphor, deep and surface anaphors (see Chapter 7), and representations of text con-tent and text form, the simple processing theory put forward by those authors (Sag & Hankamer, 1984) is incorrect. Sag and Hankamer proposed that deep anaphors are interpreted directly from a mental model and that sur-face anaphors are interpreted by copying part of a superficial representa-tion (logical form). However, experimental research suggests that both types of representation are used to interpret both types of anaphor. The language processing system is opportunistic, and will use whatever informa-tion is available to it. Sometimes it may arrive at an interpretation of a text, even though it also detects that the form of the text is inappropriate, for example because it breaks the parallelism constraint on surface anaphors and their antecedents. In addition, because representations of superficial form tend to be short-lived, they play a more important role in comprehen-sion when an anaphoric expression is near to its antecedent than when it is further away.

FOCUS

Many anaphoric expressions have little semantic content of their own, and provide few constraints on their interpretation. So, most of the constraints on interpretation must come from context (as represented, at least in part, in the mental model). A mental model of a text will contain representations of only a few individuals, but even that set may not be small enough to constrain the interpretation of, say, a definite pronoun such as "it". Mental models must, therefore, be partitioned so that only a restricted set of individuals, often only one, is a likely referent for a singular definite pronoun. The details of how such partitioning occurs, and how many partitions are necessary to account for the interpretation of different types of anaphoric expression, remain to be worked out, but many of the factors that affect partitioning, such as status of characters (e.g., main versus subordinate) and episode boundaries, have been investigated.

The idea that there is one and only one candidate for pronominal reference at any point in a text is another attractive, but incorrect one. When there is more than one candidate, other factors must contribute to the interpretation of an anaphoric expression. These factors include matching on features such as gender, at either the morphosyntactic or semantic level, and knowledge-based inferences such as those that underlie judgements of implicit causality (see Chapter 9) or stereotyping (see Chapter 10).

INFERENCE

Inferences are also needed in other cases of anaphor interpretation, particularly when no suitable meaning can be computed straightforwardly, for example by making a definite pronoun co-referential with a recent noun phrase. E-type pronouns (see Chapter 4) and pronouns that refer into anaphoric islands (see Chapter 8) require inferences for their interpretation, as do anaphoric definite noun phrases that have to be linked to things represented in a mental model by bridging inferences. Inferences depend on knowledge about the world, and mental models theory explains how such background knowledge can be integrated with information in a text representation. Since mental models represent situations in real, fictional, and abstract worlds, they are similar in form to long-term memory representations of those worlds.

An important general question about text comprehension is what inferences are made and when. One suggestion is that only those inferences that are required for a coherent interpretation of a text are made. That is to say, inferences are made in a backwards direction when they are needed to link information in different parts of a text. In the study of anaphor interpretation there is some evidence that inferences linked to stereotypes (see Chapter 10) and, possibly anaphoric islands (see Chapter 8) may be made in a forwards direction, before they are needed to establish coherence. However, as the discussion in those chapters shows, such claims can be difficult to substantiate.

SUMMARY

Mental models are a crucial component of the theory of text comprehension, and they play a central role in the interpretation of anaphoric expressions. However, the interpretation of anaphors may also depend to a greater (for ellipses) or lesser extent on representations of surface form. Nevertheless, anaphoric expressions are always correctly interpreted as referring to things in the world represented in the mental model of the text in which they occur. Even though mental models contain representations of a restricted part of a world, they must be partitioned to account for how semantically highly attenuated expressions, such as definite pronouns, are interpreted. Inferences are an important component of text comprehension, and are often needed to interpret anaphoric expressions. Mental models theory provides a framework within which inference making can readily be accommodated.

References

Albrecht, J.E., & Clifton, C., Jr. (1998). Accessing singular antecedents in conjoined phrases. *Memory & Cognition, 26*, 599–610.

Albrecht, J.E., & Myers, J.L. (1998). Accessing distant text information during reading: Effects of contextual cues. *Discourse Processes, 26*, 87–107.

Almor, A. (1999). Noun-phrase anaphora and focus: The informational load hypothesis. *Psychological Review, 106*, 748–765.

Anderson, A., Garrod, S.C., & Sanford, A.J. (1983). The accessibility of pronominal antecedents as a function of episode shifts in narrative text. *Quarterly Journal of Experimental Psychology, 35A*, 427–440.

Anderson, J.R. (1983). *The architecture of cognition*. Cambridge, MA: Harvard University Press.

Anderson, R.C., Pichert, J.W., Goetz, E.T., Schallert, D.L., Stevens, K.V., & Trollip, S.R. (1976). Instantiation of general terms. *Journal of Verbal Learning and Verbal Behavior, 15*, 667–679.

Ariel, M. (1990). *Accessing noun-phrase antecedents*. London: Routledge.

Asher, N. (1993). *Reference to abstract objects in discourse*. Dordrecht, The Netherlands: Kluwer Academic Publishers.

Asher, N., & Lascarides, A. (1998). Bridging. *Journal of Semantics, 15*, 83–113.

Au, T.K. (1986). A verb is worth a thousand words: The causes and consequences of interpersonal events implicit in language. *Journal of Memory and Language, 25*, 104–122.

Bach, E., & Partee, B.H. (1980). Anaphora and semantic structures. In J. Kreiman & A. Ojeda (Eds.), *Papers from the parasession on anaphora*. Chicago: Chicago Linguistics Society.

Banaji, M.R., & Hardin, C.D. (1996). Automatic stereotyping. *Psychological Science, 7*, 136–141.

Bannister, D. (1983). *Burning leaves*. London: Pan.

Barwise, J., & Perry, J. (1983). *Situations and attitudes*. Cambridge, MA: MIT Press/Bradford Books.

Bever, T.G., & Townsend, D.J. (1979). Perceptual mechanisms and formal properties of main and subordinate clauses. In W.E. Cooper & E.C.T. Walker (Eds.), *Sentence processing:*

Psycholinguistic studies presented to Merrill Garrett (pp. 159–226). Hillsdale, NJ: Lawrence Erlbaum Associates Inc.

Bolinger, D. (1979). Pronouns in discourse. In T. Givón (Ed.), *Syntax and semantics: Vol. 12. Discourse and syntax* (pp. 289–309). New York: Academic Press.

Bosch, P. (1983). *Agreement and anaphora: A study of the role of pronouns in syntax and discourse.* London: Academic Press.

Bosch, P. (1987). Pronouns under control? A reply to Liliane Taskowski and Paul Verluyten. *Journal of Semantics, 5,* 65–78.

Bransford, J.D., Barclay, J.R., & Franks, J.J. (1972). Sentence memory: A constructive vs interpretive approach. *Cognitive Psychology, 3,* 193–209.

Bransford, J.D., & Franks, J.J. (1971). The abstraction of linguistic ideas. *Cognitive Psychology, 2,* 331–350.

Brown, R., & Fish, D. (1983). The psychological causality implicit in language. *Cognition, 14,* 237–273.

Brown, G., & Yule, G. (1983). *Discourse analysis.* Cambridge: Cambridge University Press.

Browne, W. (1974). On the topology of anaphoric peninsulars. *Linguistic Inquiry, 5,* 619–620.

Cacciari, C., Carreiras, M., & Cionini, C.B. (1997). When words have two genders: Anaphor resolution for Italian functionally ambiguous words. *Journal of Memory and Language, 37,* 517–532.

Caenepeel, M. (1989). *Aspect, temporal ordering and perspective in narrative fiction.* Unpublished PhD thesis, University of Edinburgh, UK.

Cann, R. (1993). *Formal semantics: An introduction.* Cambridge, UK: Cambridge University Press.

Caramazza, A., Grober, E., Garvey, C., & Yates, J. (1977). Comprehension of anaphoric pronouns. *Journal of Verbal Learning and Verbal Behavior, 16,* 601–609.

Caramazza, A., & Gupta, S. (1979). The roles of topicalization, parallel function and verb semantics in the interpretation of pronouns. *Linguistics, 17,* 497–518.

Carreiras, M. (1997). Plural pronouns and the representation of their antecedents. *European Journal of Cognitive Psychology, 9,* 53–87.

Carreiras, M., Garnham, A., & Oakhill, J.V. (1993). The use of superficial and meaning-based representations in interpreting pronouns: Evidence from Spanish. *European Journal of Cognitive Psychology, 5,* 93–116.

Carreiras, M., Garnham, A., Oakhill, J.V., & Cain, K. (1996). The use of stereotypical gender information in constructing a mental model: Evidence from English and Spanish. *Quarterly Journal of Experimental Psychology, 49A,* 639–663.

Chambers, C.G., & Smyth, R.H. (1998). Structural parallelism and discourse coherence: A test of centering theory. *Journal of Memory and Language, 39,* 593–608.

Chomsky, N. (1965). *Aspects of the theory of syntax.* Cambridge, MA: MIT Press.

Chomsky, N. (1968). *Language and mind.* New York: Harcourt, Brace, Jovanovitch.

Chomsky, N. (1981). *Lectures on government and binding.* Dordrecht, The Netherlands: Foris.

Chomsky, N. (1986). *Knowledge of language: Its nature, origin and use.* New York: Praeger.

Chung, S., Ladusaw, W., & McCloskey, J. (1995). Sluicing and logical form. *Natural Language Semantics, 3,* 239–282.

Clark, H.H. (1977). Bridging. In P.N. Johnson-Laird & P.C. Wason (Eds.), *Thinking: Readings in cognitive science* (pp. 411–420). Cambridge, UK: Cambridge University Press.

Clark, H.H., & Sengul, C.J. (1979). In search of referents for noun phrases and pronouns. *Memory and Cognition, 7,* 35–41.

Clifton, C., Jr., & Ferreira, F. (1987). Discourse structure and anaphora: Some experimental results. In M. Coltheart (Ed.), *Attention and performance XII: The psychology of reading* (pp. 635–654). Hove, UK: Lawrence Erlbaum Associates Ltd.

Clifton, C., Jr., Kennison, S.M., & Albrecht, J.E. (1997). Reading the words *her, his, him:*

Implications for parsing principles based on frequency and on structure. *Journal of Memory and Language, 36,* 276–292.

Cloitre, M., & Bever, T.G. (1988). Linguistic anaphors, levels of representation, and discourse. *Language and Cognitive Processes, 3,* 293–322.

Corbett, A.T. (1984). Pronominal adjectives and the disambiguation of anaphoric noun phrases. *Journal of Verbal Learning and Verbal Behavior, 23,* 683–695.

Corbett, A.T., & Chang, F.R. (1983). Pronoun disambiguation: Accessing potential antecedents. *Memory and Cognition, 11,* 283–294.

Corbett, A.T., & Dosher, B.A. (1978). Instrument inferences in sentence encoding. *Journal of Verbal Learning and Verbal Behavior, 17,* 479–491.

Cornish, F. (1988). Anaphoric pronouns: Under linguistic control of signalling particular discourse representations? *Journal of Semantics, 5,* 233–260.

Cornish, F. (1996). "Antecedentless" anaphors: Deixis, anaphora, or what? *Journal of Linguistics, 32,* 19–41.

Cornish, F. (1999). *Anaphora, discourse, and understanding: Evidence from English and French.* Oxford, UK: Oxford University Press.

Corum, C. (1973). Anaphoric peninsulas. *Chicago Linguistics Society, 9,* 89–97.

Cowan, J.R. (1980). The significance of parallel function in the assignment of anaphora. In J. Kreiman & A.E. Ojeda (Eds.), Papers from the parasession on pronouns and anaphora (pp. 110–124). Chicago: Chicago Linguistics Society.

Cowart, W., & Cairns, H.S. (1987). Evidence for an anaphoric mechanism within syntactic processing: Some reference relations defy semantic and pragmatic constraints. *Memory and Cognition, 15,* 318–331.

Craik, K. (1943). *The nature of explanation.* Cambridge, UK: Cambridge University Press.

Crawley, R.A., Stevenson, R.J., & Kleinman, D. (1990). The use of heuristic strategies in the interpretation of pronouns. *Journal of Psycholinguistic Research, 19,* 245–264.

Crinean, M., & Garnham, A. (1999). *The relationship between implicit causality, implicit consequentiality and semantic roles.* Unpublished manuscript, Laboratory of Experimental Psychology, University of Sussex, UK.

Davidson, D. (1967). The logical form of action sentences. In N. Rescher (Ed.), *The logic of decision and action* (pp. 81–95). Pittsburgh, PA: University of Pittsburgh Press.

Dell, G.S., McKoon, G., & Ratcliff, R. (1983). The activation of antecedent information during the processing of anaphoric reference in reading. *Journal of Verbal Learning and Verbal Behavior, 22,* 121–132.

Duffy, S.A., & Keir, J.A. (1998, November). *Violating stereotypes: Comprehension processes when text conflicts with world knowledge.* Poster presented at the 39th annual meeting of the Psychonomic Society, Dallas, TX.

Edwards, D., & Potter, J. (1993). Language and causation: A discursive action model of description and attribution. *Psychological Review, 100,* 23–41.

Ehrlich, K. (1980). Comprehension of pronouns. *Quarterly Journal of Experimental Psychology, 32,* 247–255.

Ehrlich, K. (1983). Eye movements in pronoun assignment: A study of sentence integration. In K. Rayner (Ed.), *Eye movements in reading: Perceptual and language processes* (pp. 253–268). New York: Academic.

Ehrlich, K., & Rayner, K. (1983). Pronoun assignment and semantic integration during reading: Eye movements and immediacy of processing. *Journal of Verbal Learning and Verbal Behavior, 22,* 75–87.

Evans, G. (1980). Pronouns. *Linguistic Inquiry, 11,* 337–362.

Fiengo, R., & May, R. (1994). *Indices and identity.* Cambridge, MA: MIT Press.

Fillenbaum, S., & Rapoport, A. (1971). *Structures in the subjective lexicon.* New York: Academic Press.

Fillenbaum, S., & Rapoport, A. (1974). Verbs of judging, judged: A case study. *Journal of Verbal Learning and Verbal Behavior*, *13*, 54–62.

Fillmore, C.J. (1968). The case for case. In E. Bach & R.T. Harms (Eds.), *Universals in linguistic theory* (pp. 1–87). New York: Holt, Rinehart & Winston.

Fillmore, C.J. (1971). Verbs of judging: An exercise in semantic description. In C.J. Fillmore & D.T. Langendoen (Eds.), *Studies in linguistic semantics* (pp. 273–296). New York: Holt, Rinehart & Winston.

Fillmore, C.J. (1977). The case for case reopened. In P. Cole & J.M. Sadock (Eds.), *Syntax and semantics: Vol. 8. Grammatical relations* (pp. 59–81). New York: Academic Press.

Fletcher, C.R., & Bloom, C.P. (1988). Causal reasoning in the comprehension of simple narrative texts. *Journal of Memory and Language*, *27*, 235–244.

Fodor, J.A. (1983). *The modularity of mind*. Cambridge, MA: MIT Press/Bradford Books.

Fodor, J.A., Bever, T.G., & Garrett, M.F. (1974). *The psychology of language: An introduction to psycholinguistics and generative grammar*. New York: McGraw-Hill.

Foss, B. (1986). Review of A. Reber *Dictionary of Psychology. Bulletin of the British Psychological Society*, *39*, 250–251.

Fox, B.A. (1987). *Discourse structure and anaphora: Written and conversational English*. Cambridge, UK: Cambridge University Press.

Frazier, L., & Clifton, C., Jr. (1998). Comprehension of sluiced sentences. *Language and Cognitive Processes*, *13*, 499–520.

Frederiksen, J.R. (1981). Understanding anaphora: Rules used by readers in assigning pronominal reference. *Discourse Processes*, *4*, 323–347.

Garnham, A. (1979). Instantiation of verbs. *Quarterly Journal of Experimental Psychology, 31*, 207–214.

Garnham, A. (1981). Anaphoric reference to instances, instantiated and non-instantiated categories: A reading-time study. *British Journal of Psychology*, *72*, 377–384.

Garnham, A. (1984). Effects of specificity on the interpretation of anaphoric noun phrases. *Quarterly Journal of Experimental Psychology*, *36A*, 1–12.

Garnham, A. (1987). Effects of antecedent distance and intervening text structure in the interpretation of ellipses. *Language and Speech*, *30*, 59–68.

Garnham, A. (1989a). A unified theory of the meaning of some spatial relational terms. *Cognition*, *31*, 45–60.

Garnham, A. (1989b). Integrating information in text comprehension: The interpretation of anaphoric noun-phrases. In G. Carlson & M. Tanenhaus (Eds.), *Linguistic structure in language processing* (pp. 359–399). Dordrecht, The Netherlands: Kluwer Academic Publishers.

Garnham, A. (1991). Where does coherence come from? A psycholinguistic perspective. *Occasional Papers in Systemic Linguistics*, *5*, 131–141.

Garnham, A. (1992). Minimalism versus constructionism: A false dichotomy in theories of inference during reading. PSYCOLOQUY, *3*(63), Reading Inference, 1.1.

Garnham, A. (1993). Is logicist cognitive science possible? *Mind and Language*, *8*, 49–71.

Garnham, A. (1994). Future directions. In M.A. Gernsbacher (Ed.), *Handbook of psycholinguistics* (pp. 1123–1144). San Diego: Academic Press.

Garnham, A. (1996). The other side of mental models: Theories of language comprehension. In J.V. Oakhill & A. Garnham (Eds.), *Mental models in cognitive science: Essays in honour of Phil Johnson-Laird* (pp. 35–52). Hove, UK: Psychology Press.

Garnham, A., & Oakhill, J.V. (1985). On-line resolution of anaphoric pronouns: Effects of inference making and verb semantics. *British Journal of Psychology*, *76*, 385–393.

Garnham, A., & Oakhill, J.V. (1987). Interpreting elliptical verb phrases. *Quarterly Journal of Experimental Psychology*, *39A*, 611–627.

Garnham, A., & Oakhill, J.V. (1988). "Anaphoric islands" revisited. *Quarterly Journal of Experimental Psychology*, *40A*, 719–735.

Garnham, A., Oakhill, J.V., & Cain, K. (1997). The interpretation of anaphoric noun phrases: Time course, and effects of overspecificity. *Quarterly Journal of Experimental Psychology*, *50A*, 149–162.

Garnham, A., Oakhill, J.V., & Cain, K. (1998). Selective retention of information about the superficial form of text: Ellipses with antecedents in main and subordinate clauses. *Quarterly Journal of Experimental Psychology*, *51A*, 19–39.

Garnham, A., Oakhill, J.V., & Cruttenden, H. (1992). The role of implicit causality and gender cue in the interpretation of pronouns. *Language and Cognitive Processes*, *7*, 231–255.

Garnham, A., Oakhill, J.V., Ehrlich, M.-F., & Carreiras, M. (1995). Representations and processes in the interpretation of pronouns: New evidence from Spanish and French. *Journal of Memory and Language*, *34*, 41–62.

Garnham, A., Oakhill, J.V., & Reynolds, D.J. (2000). *References into anaphoric islands: Backward or forward inferences?* Unpublished manuscript, Laboratory of Experimental Psychology, University of Sussex, UK.

Garnham, A., Traxler, M., Oakhill, J.V., & Gernsbacher, M.A. (1996). The locus of implicit causality effects in comprehension. *Journal of Memory and Language*, *35*, 517–543.

Garrod, S.C., Freudenthal, D., & Boyle, E. (1994). The role of different types of anaphor in the on-line resolution of sentences in a discourse. *Journal of Memory and Language*, *33*, 39–68.

Garrod, S.C., O'Brien, E.J., Morris, R.K., & Rayner, K. (1990). Elaborative inferencing as an active or passive process. *Journal of Experimental Psychology: Learning, Memory, and Cognition*, *16*, 250–257.

Garrod, S.C., & Sanford, A.J. (1977). Interpreting anaphoric relations: The integration of semantic information while reading. *Journal of Verbal Learning and Verbal Behavior*, *16*, 77–90.

Garrod, S.C., & Sanford, A.J. (1981). Bridging inferences and the extended domain of reference. In J. Long & A. Baddeley (Eds.), *Attention and performance IX* (pp. 331–346). Hillsdale, NJ: Lawrence Erlbaum Associates Inc.

Garrod, S.C., & Sanford, A.J. (1982). The mental representation of discourse in a focussed memory system: Implications for the interpretation of anaphoric noun phrases. *Journal of Semantics*, *1*, 21–41.

Garrod, S.C., & Sanford, A.J. (1985). On the real-time character of interpreting during reading. *Language and Cognitive Processes*, *1*, 43–61.

Garrod, S.C., & Sanford, A.J. (1994). Resolving sentences in a discourse context: How discourse representation affects language understanding. In M.A. Gernsbacher (Ed.), *Handbook of psycholinguistics* (pp. 675–698). San Diego, CA: Academic Press.

Garvey, C., & Caramazza, A. (1974). Implicit causality in verbs. *Linguistic Inquiry*, *5*, 459–464.

Garvey, C., Caramazza, A., & Yates, J. (1975). Factors influencing assignment of pronoun antecedents. *Cognition*, *3*, 227–243.

Geach, P. (1962). *Reference and generality*. Ithaca, NY: Cornell University Press.

Gernsbacher, M.A. (1989). Mechanisms that improve referential access. *Cognition*, *32*, 99–156.

Gernsbacher, M.A. (1990). *Language comprehension as structure building*. Hillsdale, NJ: Lawrence Erlbaum Associates Inc.

Gernsbacher, M.A. (1991). Comprehending conceptual anaphors. *Language and Cognitive Processes*, *6*, 81–105.

Gernsbacher, M.A., & Hargreaves, D. (1988). Accessing sentence participants: The advantage of first mention. *Journal of Memory and Language*, *27*, 699–717.

Gernsbacher, M.A., & Hargreaves, D. (1992). The privilege of primacy: Experimental data and cognitive explanations. In D.L. Payne (Ed.), *Pragmatics of word order flexibility* (pp. 83–116). Philadelphia: John Benjamins.

Gerrig, R.J. (1986). Process models and pragmatics. In N.E. Sharkey (Ed.), *Advances in cognitive science* (pp. 23–42). Chichester, UK: Ellis Horwood.

Glenberg, A.M., & Swanson, N.C. (1986). A temporal distinctiveness theory of recency and modality effects. *Journal of Experimental Psychology: Learning, Memory and Cognition, 12*, 3–15.

Goldman, S.R. (1997). Learning from text: Reflections on 20 years of research and suggestions for new directions of inquiry. *Discourse Processes, 23*, 357–398.

Gordon, P.C., & Chan, D. (1995). Pronouns, passives, and discourse coherence. *Journal of Memory and Language, 34*, 216–231.

Gordon, P.C., Grosz, B.J., & Gilliom, L.A. (1993). Pronouns, names, and the centering of attention. *Cognitive Science, 17*, 311–347.

Gordon, P.C., & Hendrick, R. (1997). Intuitive knowledge of linguistic coreference. *Cognition, 62*, 325–370.

Gordon, P.C., & Hendrick, R. (1998). The representation and processing of coreference in discourse. *Cognitive Science, 22*, 389–424.

Gordon, P.C., & Hendrick, R. (1999). Nondefinite NP anaphora: A reappraisal. *Chicago Linguistics Society, 34*, 195–210.

Gordon, P.C., Hendrick, R., & Ledoux, K. (1998, November). *Language comprehension and probe-word memory*. Paper presented at the 39th annual meeting of the Psychonomic Society, Dallas, TX.

Gordon, P.C., Hendrick, R., Ledoux, K., & Yang, C.L. (1999). Processing of reference and the structure of language: An analysis of complex noun phrases. *Language and Cognitive Processes, 14*, 353–379.

Gordon, P.C., & Scearce, K.A. (1995). Pronominalization and discourse coherence, discourse structure and pronoun interpretation. *Memory & Cognition, 23*, 131–323.

Graesser, A.C., Singer, M., & Trabasso, T. (1994). Constructing inferences during narrative text comprehension. *Psychological Review, 101*, 371–395.

Green, D.W., Mitchell, D.C., & Hammond, E.J. (1981). The scheduling of text integration processes in reading. *Quarterly Journal of Experimental Psychology, 33A*, 455–464.

Greene, S.B., Gerrig, R.J., McKoon, G., & Ratcliff, R. (1994). Unheralded pronouns and management by common ground. *Journal of Memory and Language, 33*, 511–526.

Greene, S.B., McKoon, G., & Ratcliff, R. (1992). Pronoun resolution and discourse models. *Journal of Experimental Psychology: Learning Memory and Cognition, 18*, 266–283.

Grimes, J.E. (1975). *The thread of discourse*. The Hague, The Netherlands: Mouton.

Grinder, J., & Postal, P.M. (1971). Missing antecedents. *Linguistic Inquiry, 2*, 269–312.

Grober, E.H., Beardsley, W., & Caramazza, A. (1978). Parallel function in pronoun assignment. *Cognition, 6*, 117–133.

Grosz, B., Joshi, A., & Weinstein, S. (1995). Centering: A framework for modelling the local coherence of discourse. *Computational Linguistics, 21*, 203–226.

Grosz, B., & Sidner, C.L. (1986). Attentions, intentions and the structure of discourse. *Computational Linguistics, 12*, 175–204,

Gumenik, W.E. (1979). The advantage of specific terms over general terms as cues for sentence recall: Instantiation or retrieval? *Memory and Cognition, 7*, 240–244.

Hankamer, J., & Sag, I.A. (1976). Deep and surface anaphora. *Linguistic Inquiry, 7*, 391–428.

Hardt, D. (1993). *Verb phrase ellipsis: Form, meaning, and processing* (Institute for Research in Cognitive Science Report No. 93–23). Philadelphia: University of Pennsylvania.

Haviland, S.E., & Clark, H.H. (1974). What's new? Acquiring new information as a process in comprehension. *Journal of Verbal Learning and Verbal Behavior, 13*, 512–521.

Hawkins, J.A. (1978). *Definiteness and indefiniteness: A study in reference and grammaticality prediction*. London: Croom Helm.

Heider, F. (1958). *The psychology of interpersonal relations*. New York: John Wiley & Sons.

Higginbotham, J. (1995). Tensed thoughts. *Mind and Language, 10*, 226–249.

Hirst, W., & Brill, G.A. (1980). Contextual aspects of pronoun assignment. *Journal of Verbal Learning and Verbal Behavior*, *19*, 168–175.

Hobbs, J.R. (1978). Resolving pronoun references. *Lingua*, *44*, 311–338.

Hobbs, J.R. (1979). Coherence and coreference. *Cognitive Science*, *3*, 67–90.

Hobbs, J.R. (1983). Why is discourse coherent? In F. Neubauer (Ed.), *Papers in text linguistics: Vol. 38. Coherence in natural language texts*. Hamburg, Germany: Helmut Buske Verlag.

Hudson, S.B., Tanenhaus, M.K., & Dell, G.S. (1986). The effect of the discourse center on the local coherence of a discourse. In *Proceedings of the eighth annual conference of the Cognitive Science Society* (pp. 96–101). Hillsdale, NJ: Lawrence Erlbaum Associates Inc.

Isard, S.D. (1975). Changing the context. In E.L. Keenan (Ed.), *Formal semantics of natural language* (pp. 287–296). Cambridge, UK: Cambridge University Press.

Jackendoff, R.S. (1972). Gapping and related rules. *Linguistic Inquiry*, *2*, 21–35.

Jakimik, J., & Glenberg, A.M. (1990). Verbal learning meets psycholinguistics: Modality effects in the comprehension of anaphora. *Journal of Memory and Language*, *29*, 582–590.

Johnson, K. (1996). When verb phrases go missing. *Glot International*, *2*(5), 3–9.

Johnson-Laird, P.N. (1982). Propositional representations, procedural semantics and mental models. In J. Mehler, E.C.T. Walker, & M.F. Garrett (Eds.), *Perspectives on mental representation: Experimental and theoretical studies of cognitive processes and capacities* (pp. 111–131). Hillsdale, NJ: Lawrence Erbaum Associates Inc.

Johnson-Laird, P.N. (1983). *Mental models: Towards a cognitive science of language, inference, and consciousness*. Cambridge, UK: Cambridge University Press.

Johnson-Laird, P.N. (1994a). A model theory of induction. *International Studies in the Philosophy of Science*, *8*, 5–29.

Johnson-Laird, P.N. (1994b). Mental models and probabilistic thinking. *Cognition*, *50*, 189–209.

Johnson-Laird, P.N., & Bara, R. (1984). Syllogistic inference, *Cognition*, *16*, 1–61.

Johnson-Laird, P.N., & Byrne, R. (1991). *Deduction*. Hove, UK: Lawrence Erlbaum Associates Ltd.

Johnson-Laird, P.N., Byrne, R.M.J., & Schaeken, W.S. (1992). Propositional reasoning by model. *Psychological Review*, *99*, 418–439.

Johnson-Laird, P.N., & Garnham, A. (1980). Descriptions and discourse models. *Linguistics and Philosophy*, *3*, 371–393.

Johnson-Laird, P.N., Gibbs, G., & de Mowbray, J. (1978). Meaning, amount of processing, and memory for words. *Memory and Cognition*, *6*, 372–375.

Jones, E.E., & Davies, K.E. (1965). From acts to dispositions: The attribution process in person perception. In L. Berkowitz (Ed.), *Advances in experimental social psychology* (Vol. 2, pp. 219–276). New York: Academic Press.

Kamp, H. (1979). Events, instants and temporal reference. In R. Bauerle, U. Egli, & A. von Stechow (Eds.), *Semantics from different points of view* (pp. 376–417). Berlin, UK: Springer Verlag.

Kamp, H. (1981). A theory of truth and semantic representation. In J.A.G. Groenendijk, T.M.V. Janssen, & M.B.J. Stockhof (Eds.), *Formal methods in the study of language* (pp. 227–322). Amsterdam: Mathematic Centre Tracts.

Kamp, H., & Reyle, U. (1993). *From discourse to logic: Introduction to model theoretic semantics of natural language, formal logic and discourse representation theory*. Dordrecht, The Netherlands: Kluwer Academic Publishers.

Kamp, H., & Rohrer, C. (1983). Tense in texts. In R. Bauerle, C. Schwarze, & A. von Stechow (Eds.), *Meaning, use, and interpretation of language* (pp. 250–269). Berlin, Germany: Walter de Gruyter.

Karttunen, L. (1969). Pronouns and variables. *Chicago Linguistics Society*, *5*, 108–116.

Karttunen, L. (1976). Discourse referents. In J.D. McCawley (Ed.), *Syntax and semantics: Vol. 7. Notes from the linguistic underground* (pp. 363–385). New York: Academic Press.

Katz, J.J., & Fodor, J.A. (1963). The structure of a semantic theory. *Language*, *39*, 170–210.

Keenan, E.L., & Faltz, L.M. (1985). *Boolean semantics for natural language*. Dordrecht, The Netherlands: Reidel.

Kelley, H.H. (1967). Attribution theory in social psychology. In D. Levine (Ed.), *Nebraska symposium on motivation* (Vol. 15, pp. 192–238). Lincoln, NE: University of Nebraska Press.

Kennison, S.M., & Gordon, P.C. (1997). Comprehending referential expressions during reading: Evidence from eye tracking. *Discourse Processes*, *24*, 229–252.

Kerr, J.S., & Underwood, G. (1984). Fixation time on anaphoric pronouns decreases with congruity of reference. In A.G. Gale & F. Johnson (Eds.), *Theoretical and applied aspects of eye movement research* (pp. 195–202). Amsterdam: North-Holland.

Kintsch, W. (1974). *The representation of meaning in memory*. Hillsdale, NJ: Lawrence Erlbaum Associates Inc.

Kintsch, W. (1988). The role of knowledge in discourse comprehension: A construction-integration model. *Psychological Review*, *65*, 163–182.

Kintsch, W., & van Dijk, T.A. (1978). Toward a model of discourse comprehension and production. *Psychological Review*, *85*, 363–394.

Ladusaw, W.A., & Dowty, D.R. (1988). Toward a nongrammatical account of thematic roles. In W. Wilkins (Ed.), *Syntax and semantics: Vol. 21. Thematic roles* (pp. 61–73). New York: Academic Press.

Lakoff, G. (1975). Pronouns and reference. In J.D. McCawley (Ed.), *Syntax and semantics: Vol. 7. Notes from the linguistic underground* (pp. 275–335). New York: Academic Press.

Lakoff, G., & Ross, J.R. (1972). A note on anaphoric islands and causatives. *Linguistic Inquiry*, *3*, 121–125.

Langacker, R. (1969). On pronominalization and the chain of command. In D. Reibel & S. Schane (Eds.), *Modern studies in English: Readings in transformational grammar* (pp. 160–187). Englewood Cliffs, NJ: Prentice-Hall.

Lasnik, H. (1976). Remarks on coreference. *Linguistic Analysis*, *2*, 1–22.

Lesgold, A.M. (1972). Pronominalization: A device for unifying sentences in memory. *Journal of Verbal Learning and Verbal Behavior*, *11*, 316–323.

Lesgold, A.M., Roth, S.F., & Curtis, M.E. (1979). Foregrounding effects in discourse comprehension. *Journal of Verbal Learning and Verbal Behavior*, *18*, 291–308.

Levelt, W.J.M. (1984). Some perceptual limitations on talking about space. In A.J. van Doorn, W.A. van der Grind, & J.J. Koenderink (Eds.), *Limits in perception* (pp. 323–358). Utrecht, The Netherlands: VNU Science Press.

Levin, N. (1986). *Main-verb ellipsis in spoken English*. New York: Garland Publishing.

Linde, C. (1979). Focus of attention and the choice of pronouns. In T. Givón (Ed.), *Syntax and semantics: Vol. 12. Discourse and syntax* (pp. 337–354). New York: Academic Press.

Longacre, R.E. (1976). *An anatomy of speech notions*. Lisse, The Netherlands: Peter de Ritter Press.

Lucas, M.M., Tanenhaus, M.K., & Carlson, G.N. (1990). Levels of representation in the interpretation of anaphoric reference and instrument inference. *Memory and Cognition*, 18, 611–631.

MacDonald, M.C., & MacWhinney, B. (1990). Measuring inhibition and facilitation from pronouns. *Journal of Memory and Language*, *29*, 469–492.

Malt, B.C. (1985). The role of discourse structure in understanding anaphora. *Journal of Memory and Language*, *24*, 271–289.

Mann, W.C., & Thompson, S.A. (1986). Relational propositions in discourse. *Discourse Processes*, *9*, 57–90.

Marr, D. (1982). *Vision: A computational investigation into the human representation and processing of visual information*. San Francisco: Freeman.

Marslen-Wilson, W.D. (1973). Linguistic structure and speech shadowing at very short latencies. *Nature, 224*, 522–523.

Marslen-Wilson, W.D. (1975). Sentence perception as an interactive parallel process. *Science, 189*, 226–228.

Marslen-Wilson, W.D., Levy, E. & Tyler, L.K. (1982). Producing interpretable discourse: The establishment and maintenance of reference. In R.J. Jarvella & W. Klein (Eds.), *Speech, place, and action: Studies in deixis and related topics* (pp. 339–378). Chichester, UK: John Wiley & Sons.

Marslen-Wilson, W.D., Tyler, L.K., & Koster, C. (1993). Integrative effects in utterance resolution. *Journal of Memory and Language, 32*, 647–666.

Matthews, A., & Chodorow, M.S. (1988). Pronoun resolution in two-clause sentences: Effects of ambiguity, antecedent location, and depth of embedding. *Journal of Memory and Language, 27*, 245–260.

Mauner, G., Tanenhaus, M.K., & Carlson, G.N. (1995a). A note on parallelism effects in processing deep and surface verb-phrase anaphora. *Language and Cognitive Processes, 10*, 1–12.

Mauner, G., Tanenhaus, M.K., & Carlson, G.N. (1995b). Implicit arguments in sentence processing. *Journal of Memory and Language, 34*, 337–382.

May, R. (1985). *Logical form: Its structure and derivation*. Cambridge, MA: MIT Press.

McDonald, J.L. (1997, November). *Pronoun resolution: Strategic use of verb causality, gender and congruity*. Paper presented at the 38th annual meeting of the Psychonomic Society, Philadelphia.

McDonald, J.L., & MacWhinney, B. (1995). The time course of anaphor resolution: Effects of implicit verb causality and gender. *Journal of Memory and Language, 34*, 543–566.

McKoon, G., Gerrig, R.J., & Greene, S.B. (1996). Pronoun resolution without pronouns: Some consequences of memory-based text processing. *Journal of Experimental Psychology: Learning, Memory, and Cognition, 22*, 919–932.

McKoon, G., Greene, S.B., & Ratcliff, R. (1993). Discourse models, pronoun resolution, and the implicit causality of verbs. *Journal of Experimental Psychology: Learning, Memory, and Cognition, 19*, 1040–1052.

McKoon, G., & Ratcliff, R. (1980). The comprehension processes and memory structures involved in anaphoric reference. *Journal of Verbal Learning and Verbal Behavior, 19*, 668–682.

McKoon, G., & Ratcliff, R. (1990). Dimensions of inference. In A.C. Graesser & G.H. Bower (Eds.), *The psychology of learning and motivation: Vol. 25. Inferences and text comprehension* (pp. 313–328). San Diego: Academic Press.

McKoon, G., & Ratcliff, R. (1992). Inference during reading. *Psychological Review, 99*, 440–466.

McKoon, G., Ward, G., Ratcliff, R., & Sproat, R. (1993). *Journal of Memory and Language, 32*, 56–75.

Miller, G.A., & Johnson-Laird, P.N. (1976). *Language and perception*. Cambridge, UK: Cambridge University Press.

Mitchell, D.C., & Green, D.W. (1978). The effects of context and content on immediate processing in reading. *Quarterly Journal of Experimental Psychology, 28*, 325–337.

Moens, M., & Steedman, M.J. (1988). Temporal ontology and temporal reference. *Computational Linguistics, 14*, 15–28.

Monahan, K.P. (1986). *The theory of lexical phonology*. Dordrecht, The Netherlands: Reidel.

Montague, R. (1970). English as formal language. In B. Visentini et al., *Linguaggi nella società e nella tecnica* (pp. 189–224). Milan: Edizioni di Comunità.

Montague, R. (1973). The proper treatment of quantification in ordinary English. In H.J.J. Hintikka, J. Moravcsik, & P. Suppes (Eds.), *Approaches to natural language: Proceedings of the 1970 Stanford workshop on grammar and semantics* (pp. 221–242). Dordrecht, The Netherlands: Reidel.

Moxey, L.M., & Sanford, A.J. (1993). *Communicating quantities: A psychological perspective.* Hove, UK: Lawrence Erlbaum Associates Ltd.

Murphy, G.L. (1985a). Processes of understanding anaphora. *Journal of Memory and Language, 24*, 290–303.

Murphy, G.L. (1985b). Psychological explanations of deep and surface anaphora. *Journal of Pragmatics, 9*, 785–813.

Murphy, G.L. (1990). Interpretation of verb phrase anaphora: Influences of task and syntactic context. *Quarterly Journal of Experimental Psychology, 42A*, 675–692.

Myers, J.L., & Duffy, S.A. (1990). Causal inferences and text memory. In A.C. Graesser & G.H. Bower (Eds.), *The psychology of learning and motivation* (Vol. 25, pp. 159–173). San Diego, CA: Academic Press.

Nelken, R., & Francez, N. (1997). Splitting the reference time: The analogy between nominal and temporal anaphora revisited. *Journal of Semantics, 14*, 369–416.

Newell, A. (1990). *Unified theories of cognition: The 1987 William James lectures.* Cambridge, MA: Harvard University Press.

Nicol, J., & Swinney, D. (1989). The role of structure in coreference assignment during sentence processing. *Journal of Psycholinguistic Research, 18*, 5–19.

Noordman, L.G.M., & Vonk, W. (1992). Readers' knowledge and the control of inferences in reading. *Language and Cognitive Processes, 7*, 373–391.

Oakhill, J.V., & Garnham, A. (1992). Linguistic prescriptions and anaphoric reality, *Text, 12*, 161–182.

Oakhill, J.V., Garnham, A., Cain, K., & Reynolds, D.J. (2000a). *Does superficial information play a role in the interpretation of pronouns.* Unpublished manuscript, Laboratory of Experimental Psychology, University of Sussex, UK.

Oakhill, J.V., Garnham, A., Gernsbacher, M.A., & Cain, K. (1992). How natural are conceptual anaphors? *Language and Cognitive Processes, 7*, 257–280.

Oakhill, J.V., Garnham, A., & Reynolds, D.J. (2000b). *Immediate activation of stereotypical gender information during reading.* Unpublished manuscript, Laboratory of Experimental Psychology, University of Sussex, UK.

Oakhill, J.V., Garnham, A., Reynolds, D., & Wilshire, C. (1998, July). *Implicit causality effects in the interpretation of pronouns.* Poster presented at the eighth annual meeting of the Society for Text and Discourse, Madison, WI.

Oakhill, J.V., Garnham, A., & Vonk, W. (1989). The on-line construction of discourse models. *Language and Cognitive Processes, 4*, 263–286.

O'Brien, E.J. (1987). Antecedent search processes and the structure of text. *Journal of Experimental Psychology: Learning, Memory, and Cognition, 13*, 278–290.

O'Brien, E.J., & Albrecht, J.E. (1991). The role of context in accessing antecedents in text. *Journal of Experimental Psychology: Learning, Memory, and Cognition, 17*, 94–102.

O'Brien, E.J., Albrecht, J.E., Hakala, C.M., & Rizzella, M.L. (1995). Activation and suppression of antecedents during reading. *Journal of Experimental Psychology: Learning, Memory, and Cognition, 21*, 626–634.

O'Brien, E.J., Duffy, S.A., & Myers, J.L. (1986). Anaphoric inference during reading. *Journal of Experimental Psychology: Learning, Memory, and Cognition, 12*, 346–352.

O'Brien, E.J., Lorch, R.F. Jr., & Myers, J.L. (Eds.). (1998). *Memory-based text processing. Discourse Processes, 26*, 67–221.

O'Brien, E.J., Plewes, P.S., & Albrecht, J.E. (1990). Antecedent retrieval processes. *Journal of Experimental Psychology: Learning, Memory, and Cognition, 16*, 241–249.

O'Brien, E.J., Raney, G.E., Albrecht, J.E., & Rayner, K. (1997). Processes involved in the resolution of explicit anaphors. *Discourse Processes, 23*, 1–24.

O'Brien, E.J., Shanks, D.M., Myers, J.L., & Rayner, K. (1988). Elaborative inferences during reading: Do they occur online? *Journal of Experimental Psychology: Learning, Memory, and Cognition, 14*, 410–420.

Osgood, C.E. (1970). Interpersonal verbs and interpersonal behavior. In J.L. Cowan (Ed.), *Studies in thought and language* (pp. 133–228). Tucson, AZ: University of Arizona Press.

Paris, S.G., & Lindauer, B.K. (1976). The role of inference in children's comprehension and memory for sentences. *Cognitive Psychology, 8*, 217–227.

Parsons, T. (1990). *Events in the semantics of English: A study in subatomic semantics.* Cambridge, MA: MIT Press.

Partee, B. (1984). Nominal and temporal anaphora. *Linguistics and Philosophy, 7*, 243–286.

Pinker, S. (1993). The central problem for the psycholinguist. In G. Harman (Ed.), *Conceptions of the human mind: Essays in honor of George A. Miller* (pp. 59–84). Hillsdale, NJ: Lawrence Erlbaum Associates Inc.

Postal, P. (1969). Anaphoric islands. *Chicago Linguistics Society, 5*, 205–239.

Prior, A.N. (1968). *Papers on time and tense.* Oxford, UK: Clarendon Press.

Pustejovsky, J. (1995). *The generative lexicon.* Cambridge, MA: MIT Press.

Rayner, K., & Pollatsek, A. (1989). *The psychology of reading.* Englewood Cliffs, NJ: Prentice-Hall.

Rayner, K., Sereno, S.C., Morris, R.K., Schmauder, A.R., & Clifton, C., Jr. (1989). Eye-movements and on-line language comprehension processes. *Language and Cognitive Processes, 4*, SI21–49.

Reichenbach, H. (1947). *Elements of symbolic logic.* New York: Macmillan.

Reinhart, T. (1981). Definite NP-anaphora and C-command domains. *Linguistic Inquiry, 12*, 605–635.

Reinhart, T. (1983). *Anaphora and semantic interpretation.* London: Croom Helm.

Reuland, E., & Koster, J. (1991). Long-distance anaphora: An overview. In J. Koster & E. Reuland (Eds.), *Long-distance anaphora* (pp. 1–25). Cambridge, UK: Cambridge University Press.

Reynolds, D.J., Garnham, A., & Oakhill, J.V. (2000). *Evidence of immediate activation of gender information from a social role name.* Unpublished manuscript, Laboratory of Experimental Psychology, University of Sussex, UK.

Ross, J.R. (1967). *Constraints on variables in syntax.* Bloomington, IN: Indiana University Linguistics Club.

Ross, J.R. (1986). *Infinite syntax.* Norwood, NJ: Ablex.

Sadock, J.M. (1974). *Toward a linguistic theory of speech acts.* New York: Academic Press.

Sag, I.A. (1976). A logical theory of verb phrase deletion. *Chicago Linguistics Society, 12*, 533–547.

Sag, I.A., & Hankamer, J. (1984). Toward a theory of anaphoric processing. *Linguistics and Philosophy, 7*, 325–345.

Sanford, A.J. (1985a). Aspects of pronoun interpretation: Evaluation of search formulations of inference. In G. Rickheit & H. Strohner (Eds.), *Inference in text processing* (pp. 183–204). Amsterdam: North-Holland.

Sanford, A.J. (1985b). *Cognition and cognitive psychology.* London: Weidenfeld & Nicolson.

Sanford, A.J. (1987). *The mind of man: Models of human understanding.* Brighton, UK: Harvester Press.

Sanford, A.J., & Garrod, S.C. (1980). Memory and attention in text comprehension: The problem of reference. In R.S. Nickerson (Ed.), *Attention and performance VIII* (pp. 459–474). Hillsdale, NJ: Lawrence Erlbaum Associates Inc.

Sanford, A.J., & Garrod, S.C. (1981). *Understanding written language: Explorations in comprehension beyond the sentence.* Chichester, UK: John Wiley & Sons.

Sanford, A.J., & Garrod, S.C. (1989). What, when and how: Questions of immediacy in anaphoric reference resolution. *Language and Cognitive Processes, 4*, SI263–287.

Sanford, A.J., & Garrod, S.C. (1998). The role of scenario mapping in text comprehension. *Discourse Processes, 26*, 159–190.

Sanford, A.J., Garrod, S.C., Lucas, A., & Henderson, R. (1984). Pronouns without antecedents? *Journal of Semantics, 2*, 303–318.

Sanford, A.J., & Lockhart, F. (1990). Description types and method of conjoining as factors influencing plural anaphora: A continuation study of focus. *Journal of Semantics, 7*, 365–378.

Sanford, A.J., Moar, K., & Garrod, S.C. (1988). Proper names as controllers of discourse focus. *Language and Speech, 31*, 43–56.

Sanford, A.J., & Moxey, L.M. (1999). What are mental models made of? In G. Rickheit & C. Habel (Eds.), *Mental models in discourse processing and reasoning* (pp. 57–76). Amsterdam: Elsevier.

Schaeffer, B., & Wallace, R. (1969). The comparison of word meanings. *Journal of Experimental Psychology, 86*, 144–152.

Semin, G., & Fiedler, K. (1989). Relocating attributional phenomena within a language-cognition interface: The case of actors' and observers' perspectives. *European Journal of Social Psychology, 19*, 491–508.

Sheldon, A. (1974). The role of parallel function in the acquisition of relative clauses in English. *Journal of Verbal Learning and Verbal Behavior, 13*, 272–281.

Sheldon, A. (1977). On strategies for processing relative clauses: A comparison of children and adults. *Journal of Psycholinguistic Research, 6*, 305–318.

Shillcock, R. (1982). The on-line resolution of pronominal anaphora. *Language and Speech, 25*, 385–401.

Simner, J., & Garnham, A. (1999, September). *Cross-category checks in anaphor comprehension.* Poster presented at the British Psychological Society, Cognitive Section conference, York, UK.

Smith, E.E., Langston, C., & Nisbett, R.E. (1992). The case for rules in reasoning. *Cognitive Science, 16*, 1–40.

Smith, E.E., Shoben, E.J., & Rips, L.J. (1974). Structure and process in semantic memory: A featural model for semantic decisions. *Psychological Review, 81*, 214–241.

Smyth, R.H. (1992). Multiple feature matching in pronoun resolution: A new look at parallel function. In *Proceedings of the second international conference on Spoken Language Processing* (pp. 145–148). Edmonton, Canada: Priority Printing.

Smyth, R.H. (1994). Grammatical determinants of ambiguous pronoun resolution. *Journal of Psycholinguistic Research, 23*, 197–229.

Solan, L. (1983). *Pronominal reference: Child language and the theory of grammar.* Dordrecht, The Netherlands: Reidel.

Stevenson, R.J., Crawley, R.A., & Kleinman, D. (1994). Thematic roles, focus and the representation of events. *Language and Cognitive Processes, 9*, 519–548.

Stevenson, R.J., Nelson, A.W.R., & Stenning, K. (1993). Strategies in pronoun comprehension. In *Proceedings of the 15th annual conference of the Cognitive Science Society* (pp. 976–981). Hillsdale, NJ: Lawrence Erlbaum Associates Inc.

Stevenson, R.J., Nelson, A.W.R., & Stenning, K. (1995). The role of parallelism in strategies of pronoun comprehension. *Language and Speech, 38*, 393–418.

Stevenson, R.J., & Vitkovitch, M. (1986). The comprehension of anaphoric relations. *Language and Speech, 29*, 335–360.

Stewart, A.J., Pickering, M.J., & Sanford, A.J. (1998a). Implicit consequentiality. In *Proceedings of the 20th annual conference of the Cognitive Science Society* (pp. 1031–1036). Hillsdale, NJ: Lawrence Erlbaum Associates Inc.

Stewart, A.J., Pickering, M.J., & Sanford, A.J. (1998b). The relationship between implicit causality and implicit consequentiality. In *Proceedings of the 20th annual conference of the Cognitive Science Society* (p. 1266). Hillsdale, NJ: Lawrence Erlbaum Associates Inc.

Stewart, A.J., Pickering, M.J., & Sanford, A.J. (2000). The time course of the influence of implicit causality information: Focusing versus integration accounts. *Journal of Memory and Language, 42*, 423–442.

Sutherland, N.S. (1987). *Men change too*. London: Duckworth.

Tabossi, P., & Johnson-Laird, P.N. (1980). Linguistic context and the priming of semantic information. *Quarterly Journal of Experimental Psychology, 32*, 595–603.

Tanenhaus, M.K., & Carlson, G.N. (1990). Comprehension of deep and surface verbphrase anaphors. *Language and Cognitive Processes, 5*, 257–280.

Tanenhaus, M.K., Carlson, G.N., & Seidenberg, M.S. (1985). Do listeners compute linguistic representations. In D.R. Dowty, L. Karttunen, & A.M. Zwicky (Eds.), *Natural language parsing: Psychological, computational, and theoretical perspectives* (pp. 359–408). Cambridge, UK: Cambridge University Press.

Tasmowski-De Ryck, L., & Verluyten, P. (1982). Linguistic control of pronouns. *Journal of Semantics, 1*, 323–346.

Tic Douloureux, P.R.N. (1971). A note on one's privates. In A.M. Zwicky, P.H. Salus, R.I. Binnick, & A.L. Vanek (Eds.), *Studies out in left field: Defamatory essays presented to James D. McCawley* (pp. 45–52). Edmonton, Canada: Linguistic Research Incorporated.

Townsend, D.J. (1983). Thematic processing in sentences and texts. *Cognition, 13*, 223–261.

Townsend, D.J., & Bever, T.G. (1978). Interclause relations and clausal processing. *Journal of Verbal Learning and Verbal Behaviour, 17*, 509–521.

Townsend, D.J., & Bever, T.G. (1982). Natural units of representation interact during sentence comprehension. *Journal of Verbal Learning and Verbal Behaviour, 21*, 688–703.

Trabasso, T., & van den Broek, P. (1985). Causal thinking and the representation of narrative events. *Journal of Memory and Language, 24*, 612–630.

Tyler, L.K., & Marslen-Wilson, W.D. (1982). The resolution of discourse anaphors: Some on-line studies. *Text, 2*, 263–291.

van den Broek, P., & Trabasso, T. (1986). Causal networks versus goal hierarchies in summarizing text. *Discourse Processes, 9*, 1–13.

van Dijk, T.A., & Kintsch, W. (1983). *Strategies of discourse comprehension*. New York: Academic Press.

Vonk, W. (1984). Eye movements during the comprehension of pronouns. In A.G. Gale & F. Johnson (Eds.), *Theoretical and applied aspects of eye movement research* (pp. 203–212). Amsterdam: North-Holland.

Vonk, W. (1985a). On the purpose of reading and the immediacy of processing pronouns. In R. Groner, G.W. McConkie, & C. Menz (Eds.), *Eye movements and human information processing* (pp. 207–215). Amsterdam: North-Holland.

Vonk, W. (1985b). The immediacy of inferences in the understanding of pronouns. In G. Rickheit & H. Strohner (Eds.), *Inferences in text processing* (pp. 205–218). Amsterdam: North-Holland.

Vonk, W., Hustinx, L.G.M.M., & Simons, W.H.G. (1992). The use of referential expressions in structuring discourse. *Language and Cognitive Processes, 7*, 301–333.

Walker, C.H., & Yekovitch, F.R. (1987). Activation and use of script-based antecedents in anaphoric reference. *Journal of Memory and Language, 26*, 673–691.

Walker, M.A., Joshi, A.K., & Prince, E.F. (Eds.). (1997). *Centering theory in discourse*. Oxford, UK: Clarenden Press.

Ward, G., Sproat, R. & McKoon, G. (1991). A pragmatic analysis of so-called anaphoric islands. *Language, 67*, 439–474.

Webber, B.L. (1979). *A formal approach to discourse anaphora*. New York: Garland Publishing.

Wilkins, W.K. (Ed.). (1988). *Syntax and semantics: Vol. 21. Thematic relations*. San Diego, CA: Academic Press.

Williams, E. (1977). Discourse and logical form. *Linguistic Inquiry, 8*, 101–139.
Winograd, T. (1972). Understanding natural language. *Cognitive Psychology, 3*, 1–191.
Yekovitch, F.R., Walker, C.H., & Blackman, H.S. (1979). The role of presupposed and focal information in integrating sentences. *Journal of Verbal Learning and Verbal Behavior, 18*, 535–548.

Author Index

Subject Index